Contents

	Abbreviations	
	Foreword	
	Introduction	
	Chronology	5
1	Congo pre-Independence	6
2	Congolese Political Development, 1946–1959	11
3	From Independence to Crisis	17
4	Political Insurgency in Stanleyville, 1960-1961	26
5	Political and Military Insurgency in Katanga, 1960-1963	30
6	The Chinese Method in Africa: the Kwilu Rebellion	40
7	The Kivu Rebellion	47
8	Counter-insurrection in the Congo, 1964	53
9	Epilogue	64
	Bibliography	66
	Notes	71
	Acknowledgements	80
	About the Author	80

Helion & Company Limited
Unit 8 Amherst Business Centre
Budbrooke Road
Warwick
CV34 5WE
England
Tel. 01926 499 619
Email: info@helion.co.uk
Website: www.helion.co.uk
Twitter: @helionbooks
Visit our blog http://blog.helion.co.uk/

Text © Stephen Rookes 2020
Colour profiles © David Bocquelet, Anderson Subtil, Tom Cooper 2020
Maps: Anderson Subtil, Tom Cooper 2020
Photographs: : unless stated otherwise, all the photographs used in this volume have been obtained in the form of prints from the Military Museum of Hanoi and the Vietnam News Agency, in the Socialist Republic of Vietnam, which in turn sourced them from multiple official sources and news agencies abroad.

Designed and typeset by Farr out Publications, Wokingham, Berkshire
Cover design by Paul Hewitt, Battlefield Design (www.battlefield-design.co.uk)

Every reasonable effort has been made to trace copyright holders and to obtain their permission for the use of copyright material. The author and publisher apologise for any errors or omissions in this work, and would be grateful if notified of any corrections that should be incorporated in future reprints or editions of this book.

ISBN 978-1-913336-23-3

British Library Cataloguing-in-Publication Data
A catalogue record for this book is available from the British Library

All rights reserved. No part of this publication may be reproduced, stored in a retrieval system, or transmitted, in any form, or by any means, electronic, mechanical, photocopying, recording or otherwise, without the express written consent of Helion & Company Limited.

We always welcome receiving book proposals from prospective authors.

Note: In order to simplify the use of this book, all names, locations and geographic designations are as provided in *The Times World Atlas*, or other traditionally accepted major sources of reference, as of the time of described events. Correspondingly, the term 'Congo' designates the area of the former Belgian colony of the Congo Free State, granted independence as the Democratic Republic of the Congo in June 1960 and in use until 1971 when the country was renamed Republic of Zaire, which, in turn, reverted to Democratic Republic of the Congo in 1997, and which remains in use today. As such, Congo is not to be mistaken for the former French colony of Middle Congo (Moyen Congo), officially named the Republic of the Congo on its independence in August 1960, also known as Congo-Brazzaville.

Dedication
For Thomas Edward Rookes (1932-2014) and Pauline Mary McNamara (1938-2019)

Abbreviations

ABAKO	Association des Bakongo pour l'unification, la conservation et l'expansion de langue kikongo/ Bakongo Association for the unification, the conservation, and the expansion of the Kikongo language
ABIR	Anglo-Belgian India Rubber Company
ADAPES	Association des Anciens Elèves des Pères de Scheut
AKTAR	Association of Tshokwe of Katanga and Rhodesia
ALMOKAT	Association des Originaires du Luapala Moero Katanga
ANC	Armée Nationale Congolaise
APIC	Association du personnel indigène de la colonie
APL	Armée Populaire de Libération
APS	Aborigines' Protection Society
APRON	Aerial Port Squadron
ASSANEF	Association des Anciens Elèves des Frères Chrètiens
ASSOBAKO	Association des Bahemba de Kongolo
ASSOBAKAT	Association des Basonge du Katanga
BALUBAKAT	Association des Baluba de Katanga
BCK	Compagnie du Chemin de Fer du Bas-Congo au Katanga
BKC	Belgian Katanga Company/Compagnie du Katanga
BSAC	British South African Company
BSP	Belgian Socialist Party
CABDA	Comité d'action et de défense des Belges d'Afrique
CAF	Central African Federation
CCCI	Compagnie du Congo pour le Commerce et l'Industrie
CCFC	Compagnie du Chemin de Fer du Congo
CFRB	Corps Franc Roi Baudouin
CEREA	Centre de Regroupement Africain
CIA	Central Intelligence Agency
CINSTRIKE	Commander in Chief, United States Strike Forces
CK	Katanga Company
CSK	Special Committee of the Katanga
CNL	Conseil National de Libération
CNL-B	Conseil National de Libération-Bocheley
CNL-G	Conseil National de Libération-Gbenye
COMISH	United States Military Mission, Congo
CONACO	Convention Nationale Congolaise
CONAKAT	Conféderation des associations tribales du Katanga
CRISP	Centre de Recherche et d'Information
CSK	Comité Spécial du Katanga
DCI	Director of Central Intelligence
DRC	Democratic Republic of the Congo
FAC	Force Aérienne Congolaise
FAK	Force Aérienne Katanganaise
FAR	Cuban Revolutionary Army
FATAC	Force Aérienne Tactique Congolaise
FEDEKA	Fédération des Associations de Ressortissants du Kasaï au Katanga
FETRIKAT	Fédération des Tribus du Haut-Katanga
FKL	Forces Katangaises Libres
FLN	Front de Libération Nationale
FP	Force Publique
FRUS	Foreign Relations of the United States
IAA	International African Association
JSSC	Joint Strategic Survey Council
LMS	London Missionary Society
MAP	Military Assistance Program
MATS	Military Air Transport Service
MBSOG	Maritime Branch of the Special Operations Group
MISTEBEL	Mission Technique Belge au Katanga
MNC	Mouvement National Congolais
MNC-K	Mouvement National Congolais-Kalonji
MNC-L	Mouvement National Congolais-Lumumba
MPLA	People's Movement for the Liberation of Angola
MRR	Movimento de Recuperacion Revolucionario
NAACP	National Association for the Advancement of Coloured People
NSC	National Security Council
OAS	Organisation of American States
OAU	Organisation of African Unity
PAF	Pan-African Federation
PNCP	Parti Nationale de la Convention du Peuple
PRC	People's Republic of China
PSA	Parti Solidaire Africain/African Solidarity Party
PSA-G	Parti Solidaire Africain-Gizenga
RGS	Royal Geographical Society
ROC	Republic of the Congo
SAAF	South African Air Force
SABENA	Société Anonyme Belge d'Exploitation de la Navigation Aérienne
SAD	Special Activities Division
SGB	Société Générale de Belgique
SNETA	Société Nationale pour l'Etude des Transports Aériens
SOE	Special Operations Executive
STRICOM	United States Strike Command
TAC	Tactical Air Command
TCL	Tanganyika Concessions Limited
UAR	United Arab Republic
UBWAKA	Union des Bwami des Basumbwa-Bayeke
UCOL	Union pour la colonisation du Katanga
UDA	Union Démocratique Africaine
UK	Union Katanganaise
UMHK	Union Minière du Haut-Katanga
UN	United Nations
UNAMIL	Union des anciens élèves de la mission Leverville
UNAR	Rwandan National Union
UNATRA	Union Nationale des Transports Fluviaux

UNELMA	Union des Anciens Elèves des Frères Maristes	**USAF**	United States Air Force
UNIP	United National Independence Party	**USIA**	United States Information Agency
UNISCO	Union des Intérêts Sociaux Congolais	**USEUCOM**	US European Command
UNOC	United Nations Operations in the Congo	**USSR**	Union of Soviet Socialist Republics

Foreword

Attempts to record the brutal and tragic de-colonization of Congo usually end in a remorseful, emotive recounting of difficult-to-research, previously told, superficial anecdotes strung together and presented as factual history. Stephen Rookes has made an admirable effort at the deep digging others have failed to do to uncover events that occurred in the secretive Cold War atmosphere in the years leading to, and post, independence.

In the process of analysing, sequencing, and recording these events it is difficult to avoid inadvertently taking sides with struggles and motives of those individuals who have been participants in the futile dream of unity, and viability, or those who merely sought selfish exploitation. The existential uncertainty of every aspect of what most consider 'life' has rendered the ability to make a nation from the many ethnic groups speaking different languages inherent in Congo, only a very fragile and vulnerable semblance of a nation. Rookes' diligent detailed recording of these machinations is admirable.

Communist China's Premier Zhou-enlai stated during this time that '...the key to control of Africa, is control of Congo'. The blessings of natural resources and the strategic geographical position on the African continent have been a Congo curse, a pretext for exploitation and corruption, causing inevitable environmental and human degradation, rather than for generating nation-building revenue streams. The years of brutal exploitation by King Leopold II and the Belgian government terminated in a cynical, sudden withdrawal of what national administration existed with no preparation of the Congolese for succession. In the Cold War atmosphere at independence, the absence of an educated administrative class meant there was no sense of 'nation'. The country was in reality, a non-country, when independence was achieved, despite what the United Nations proclaimed. Conditions were conducive to the Cold War manipulations which made Congo the sacrificial pawn in the grab for strategic natural resources by the great powers of the Communist World and the Free World.

Rookes has combed the range of information sources from de-classified government documents, to actual participants in these events to bring integrity to an accurate recording of events usually perverted by innocent or deliberate mis-information. His many first-hand accounts bring unprecedented authenticity.

Jim Hawes
Vietnam War veteran, former US Navy SEAL
& Head of CIA's Naval Operations in Congo

Introduction

The task of building a nation that befell Patrice Lumumba in June 1960 was decidedly unenviable. Seventy-five years after King Leopold II of Belgium had laid claim to large parts of Central Africa in moves that were to lead to the creation of the Belgian Congo, the political responsibility for over 900,000 square miles of territory was placed into Lumumba's hands overnight. Whereas regime changes can be made peacefully when the concept of the nation-state is firmly fixed in the minds of its inhabitants, in postcolonial states such as the Congo more often than not there was a divergence between urban and rural communities and between the modern and the customary. Combined with the tribal affiliations to religion and ethnicity which are still to be found in the Congo, the creation of a forward-looking hegemonic unit was always going to be difficult to accomplish without some form of social and political unrest. To complicate matters even further, the attempted creation of this unit took place within a context of global bifurcation: the east and the west were eagerly jostling to spread their respective ideologies to states where only some time beforehand their presence and influence had been minimalised. Spotting the opportunity for ideological expansion that decolonisation presented, both the east and west were willing to provide the financial and military impetus which, it was hoped, would sway support in favour of their respective ideologies and strategic objectives.

The case of the Congo in regards to these ideologies and strategies was further complicated by the abundance of high-value metals and minerals that lay on or under the country's agriculturally fertile soil. Rich, for example in diamonds, gold or high-grade uranium, the Congo's copper and land that was ideal for the production of palm oil that made it such an attractive proposition for Leopold II when the so-called 'scramble for Africa' commenced at the end of the 19th century. The reports of the large scale abuse and exploitation that filtered out of the Congo at the beginning of the 20th century persuaded Belgian authorities that King Leopold's financial ventures in Central Africa should come to an end and that the Congo should become a colony. Administered by Belgian colonial officials from 1908, the Congo benefitted from well-meaning efforts to provide educational and welfare systems. By the end of the 1950s, such had been the success of these reforms that the Congolese were among the most prosperous, well-educated and the healthiest of Africa's indigenous populations.

Be this at it may, the Congolese desire for independence from Belgium had steadily increased from 1946. Those who had been beneficiaries of the educational system began to gain a political awareness and soon they believed they were ready to follow in the footsteps of the Gold Coast and other sub-Saharan nations in obtaining the right to self-determination. Nevertheless, when independence was granted at the end of June 1960 it provided the power vacuum in which age-old and newly-born rivalries were able to express themselves not only politically but also militarily. Over the next seven years, the Congo would become one immense battlefield.

The Congo as a theatre of the Cold War and the involvement of mercenary forces from 1960 onwards has been one of the most constant focuses for observers of the crisis. Being areas of study which are not yet fully understood and which have still to reveal all their secrets, they remain highly productive for researchers, students and war buffs alike. Despite a large number of all manner of works having been published on subjects related to the Congo Crisis, two of its most interesting aspects appear to have been overlooked: somewhat surprisingly, the role of the Congolese themselves has tended to have been examined from a purely political point of view; and even more surprisingly, the role of the United States has tended to be underestimated from a military point of view. The objective of this two-volume series is to address these issues.

With this in mind, the aim of the first book in the series entitled *Ripe for Rebellion: Political and Military Insurgency in the Congo, 1946-1964* will be to throw light on the complexities of Congolese society as a whole in order to understand how the crisis was fermented historically, politically and ethnically and how the divisions generated by considerations such as these were expressed through armed warfare. Effectively, one thing that needs to be understood when examining the Congo Crisis is that it did not start with the Congo's independence, with the secession of Katanga or with the assassination of Lumumba. Though these events severely worsened and transformed localised conflict into countrywide unrest, the seeds of conflict were planted as soon as the Congolese acquired political awareness, and as soon as the Congo became a centre of interest for foreign powers from 1946. This volume takes us into the heart of the development of this political awareness; places it in the context of decolonisation and the Cold War; then explores the tribal connections, highways and byways which led to sustained military conflict until 1964. Though this date does not denote the end of the crisis nor the implication of Congolese non-state forces, what it does do is to signal the beginning of a period during which United States involvement in the crisis intensified from a military point of view. The second volume in the series entitled *For God and the CIA: Cuban Exile Forces in the Congo, 1962-1967* therefore takes up the mantle and delves into the nature of US military participation. As the terms used in the title of this volume indicate, the military participation in question was covert and involved non-US nationals. Apart from Cuban exiles having no discernible link to the Congo, what is particularly interesting is that we will see how the Congo's future was determined in part not by the Congolese themselves but by events which took place some years before the independence of the Congo and in a completely different geographical context. In addition to underlining the fatefulness attached to the Congo Crisis, this volume highlights how the CIA used a network of clandestine operations to fend off threats to US interests on a global level. Finally, the study of the involvement of Cuban exiles in the Congo provides the opportunity to ponder over the question of whether we should not be re-evaluating existing opinions on the use of mercenaries in the Congo. Whereas soldiers of fortune are seen by some as a money-hungry scourge that has no place on the field of battle, it is hoped that the example of the Cuban exiles will show that the mercenary soldier can be a force for good and that he can be an ideological warrior.

The reader will note that this work contains a substantial amount of references from both primary and secondary sources, and that the assembling of these documented and undocumented events required the use of sources which can be described as reliable or not reliable. Naturally, when dealing with undocumented sources such as personal interviews, a certain degree of caution should be exercised as recollections may, or may not be, tainted by the passage of time, by political ideologies, by personal sentiment or, in the case of veterans involved in covert operations, by the desire to protect the identities of people and places. Insofar as the question of reliability of undocumented information is concerned, when and where possible it has been cross-referenced using other official sources in order to determine its plausibility.

For other primary sources, the reader will note the frequent use of recently declassified US government documents which can be found in the archives of the US Department of State, the US Department Defence, the National Security Council, the CIA, or the United Nations. Released under the Freedom of Information Act (FOIA), an example of documents relating to US foreign policy can be found in the Foreign Relations of the United States (FRUS) series. Published under the auspices of the US Office of the Historian, this collection contains the records of presidential memorandums, conversations, diplomatic cables, or governmental reports dating back to the 19th century. Each volume of the series corresponds to a given geographical location or to a given President, and it should be noted that Volume XIII, Congo 1960-1968, declassified in 2013 was of immense help in the building of the narrative framework found in this study.

The narrative of this monograph was also aided by a substantial quantity of secondary sources available online or in physical libraries or bookshops. These range from studies which have been published in academic reviews and made available on platforms such as JSTOR, to monographs, biographies, and newspaper articles from reputable sources such *The Times*, *The Guardian*, the *Miami Herald*, and the *New York Times*.

The decision to use newspaper articles was not taken out of convenience: many of the articles were reports on the developments of the Congo Crisis prepared by war correspondents such as Lloyd Garrison or Paul Hoffman. Garrison spent much time travelling across the Congo meeting mercenary units or rebel forces, and he was to be a witness to several armed encounters. As a neutral participant in the Congo Crisis Garrison's accounts provide a highly reliable source of information.

The presence of personal blogs on the internet and the creation of pages on social media have provided an unusual but relatively productive source. As well as providing amateur historians with the means of presenting their research, reputable historians such as Jean-Pierre Sonck have created their own blogs. Naturally, when consulting this type of amateur source, a certain degree of caution should be exercised. In this respect, all references that may or may not have been used were cross-checked with other sources. The same can be said of social media platforms.

While the researcher must be careful when evaluating the degree of reliability when dealing with a source which may be jaded by the passing of time, or influenced by personal or political considerations, equally, it would be unfair, or even churlish, to completely dismiss accounts provided by the active participants of a given event.

Chronology

1482: Portuguese explorer Diego Cão becomes the first European to set foot in the Congo.
1511: The Portuguese enter the slave trade in the Congo.
1816: Captain James Tuckey investigates the possible link between the Congo and Nile basins.
1854: David Livingstone embarks on his first journey into Central Africa.
1870s: King Léopold II of Belgium provides a private venture to colonise the region known as Kongo.
1874-1877: British explorer Henry Morton Stanley explores the Congo River.
1879-1887: Stanley is commissioned by Léopold II to establish trading posts and to establish the King's authority in the Congo basin.
1884-1885: The Berlin Conference sees Léopold's authority over the Congo basin recognised.
1885: Léopold establishes the Congo Free State.
1891: The Belgians begin to colonise Katanga.
1902: Joseph Conrad's The Heart of Darkness throws light on the brutality of Léopold's regime.
1908: Following mass-killings and other atrocities, the Congo is annexed by the Belgian State. This creates the Belgian Congo.
1940s: The emergence of labour strikes in the Belgian Congo sees Belgian authority contested. This leads to a loosening of labour laws on the question of forced labour.
1950s: The emergence of Congolese national parties such as ABAKO and MNC.
1955: Van Bilsen publishes his 30-year plan for the independence of the Belgian Congo.
1959: Riots against Belgian authority take place in Léopoldville (Kinshasa).
1959: Talks are held in Belgium at the Round Table Conference to discuss the decolonisation of the Belgian Congo.
June 1960: The Democratic Republic of the Congo gains its independence.
July 1960: A mutiny by Congolese soldiers against officers of the Force Publique leads to widespread social unrest. A number of Europeans are killed in the rioting.
July 1960: Katanga secedes from the DRC and calls on Belgium for military assistance.
July 1960: The first groups of mercenaries arrive in Katanga.
August 1960: South Kasai secedes from the DRC. Lumumba reacts by appealing to the US, the USSR for help and finally asks for assistance from the UN. Peacekeeping forces arrive soon after.
September 1960: Prime Minister Patrice Lumumba is removed from power by President Joseph Kasa-Vubu who supported by Joseph Désiré Mobutu, the commanding officer of the newly-formed ANC.
December 1960: Antoine Gizenga establishes a breakaway government headquartered in Stanleyville (Kisangani) which vows to continue Lumumba's legacy.
January 1961: Lumumba is assassinated after being brutally beaten.
January 1961: More mercenaries arrive in Katanga. These include 4 Commando, and the Compagnie Internationale or White Legion.
9 February 1961: Joseph Ileo is appointed as Prime Minister of the DRC.
2 August 1961: Cyril Adoula becomes the new Prime Minister of the DRC.
13 September 1961: UN forces launch Operation Morthor to rid the Congo of mercenaries. The Siege of Jadotville sees Irish peacekeepers captured by Katangan forces.
18 September 1961: A plane carrying UN Secretary-General Dag Hammarskjöld is shot down killing all aboard.
Late 1962: The first group of Cuban Exile pilots arrives in the Congo.
Early 1963: Katangan leader Moïse Tshombe goes into exile. Katanga is reintegrated into the DRC.
Early 1963: The bulk of UN peacekeeping forces and mercenaries leave the Congo.

The Simba Rebellion

July 1963: Pierre Mulele returns from China and starts a popular revolution in the Kwilu region of the DRC.
August-September 1963: The establishment of the Conseil National de Libération (CNL).
January 1964: A state of emergency is declared in the Kwilu.
May 1964: Rebel forces led by Gaston Soumialot capture Uvira and Fizi, two towns on the northern banks of Lake Tanganyika.
June 1964: Soumialot's forces take Albertville (Kalemie).
30 June 1964: Moïse Tshombe returns to the Congo and is appointed Prime Minister.
July 1964: Mercenary units led by Mike Hoare, Jean Schramme, and Bob Denard return to the Congo at Tshombe's request.
Mid-late July 1964: Rebel forces led by Nicolas Olenga capture large portions of areas in the north and the north-west of the DRC.
Early August 1964: Olenga's troops capture Stanleyville (Kisangani). They take US diplomats hostage.
21 August 1964: The Makasi flies their first B-26 combat mission in the Congo.
September 1964: The 5th Mechanised Brigade divided into Lima I and Lima II under the command of Belgian Colonel Vandewalle begins operations to put down the rebellion.
Early September 1964: Makasi commandos led by 'Rip' Robertson arrive in the Congo.
15 September 1964: Denard's forces and the Makasi take Lisala in the north-west.
24 October 1964: Hoare's forces and the Makasi take Bumba in the north-west.
28 October 1964: Olenga orders the arrest of all Americans and Belgians in Stanleyville.
1 November 1964: The Stanleyville Column advances northwards to Kindu.
18 November 1964: Belgian paratroopers arrive in Ascension to prepare for rescue operations.

21 November 1964: The rescue operations are authorised by Congolese authorities.
22 November 1964: The Dragon Force arrives at Kamina air base.
25 November 1964: Dragon Noir operations free hostages at Isiro.
29 November 1964: Belgian paratroopers leave for Ascension.
January 1965: Operations White Giant and Violettes Impériales bring rebel operations to a standstill.
April 1965: Ernesto Guevara arrives in Tanzania.
August 1965: The Makasi naval force begins operations on Lake Tanganyika.
November 1965: Guevara's campaign comes to an end.
24 November 1965: A military takeover sees Mobutu become President of the DRC.

Table 1: Name-change of Congolese cities/towns

Name since circa 1960	Belgian Name
Bandandu	Benningville
Bukavu	Costermansville
Ilebo	Port-Francqui
Isiro	Paulis
Kananga	Luluabourg
Likasi	Jadotville
Lubumbashi	Elisabethville
Kinshasa	Léopoldville
Kisingani	Stnaleyville
Kalemie	Albertville
Kindu	Port de Kindu
Lusanga	Leverville
Mbandaka	Coquihatville
Mbanza-Ngungu	Thysville
Mbuji-Mayi	Bakwanga
Moba	Baudouinville

1
Congo pre-Independence

Sent to explore the Congo River by King John II in 1482, Portuguese navigator Diego Cão set foot in a land of varied contours and topography. From luxuriant savannas, mosquito-infested swamps to dense rainforests, snow-covered mountains and volcanoes, the Congo contained 15 cultural regions and over 250 different ethnic groups. Living as part of small communities, the Balunda, Baluba, Bakongo or Batwa peoples communicated using linguistic variations and dialects of Sudanic, Nigritic or Bantu, the most widely spoken of all the languages in the Congo. Polygamy and cannibalism were common features of societies that hunted, fished or cultivated the land and life for villagers was governed by traditions and customs passed down by the elders and chiefs. Sometimes, as is the case with the Ababua people, there was no supreme chief, and tribes lived autonomously in a defined geographical area. Within each tribe there were a number of groups each with ownership of the territory occupied by the whole tribe. Called *etina* in the local language, these groups were often subdivided into clans, or *makèré*. Each clan had its own set of laws, and any dispute between clan members was arbitrated by a council which deliberated using the basis of custom.[1]

One of the earliest examples of the way small social formations grew into much larger communities is that of the Kingdom of the Kongo. Ruled by the Kikongo-speaking House of Kilukeni since the end of the 14th century, the existence of the kingdom came about through an alliance of the Mpenba Kasi and the Mbata tribes.[2] The kingdom covered areas of western Congo and parts of current-day northern Angola and activities were centred on its capital Mbanza Kongo, later named San Salvador by the Portuguese. A significant preoccupation for rulers of the kingdom such as Henrique I Nerika a Mpudi or King Alvaro I was ensuring that the lands it occupied remained safe from attack from rival kingdoms. Examples that serve to illustrate this type of attack are the wars against the Bateke from the neighbouring Anziku Kingdom[3] or the invasion of the Jaga which took place shortly after Alvaro came to the throne in 1567. The latter was the most serious assault on Kikongo authority as the Jaga managed to capture San Salvador and badly disrupt an economic activity on which the kingdom had thrived since its inception, i.e. slavery.

The kingdom's trade in human commodity had increased gradually through its ability to defeat its rivals in battle and to use those captured as slaves. However, once the Portuguese became involved from 1511, and huge financial gains could be made as demand for slaves developed, forays were carried out into the rural regions surrounding the kingdom in order to fuel their needs. Up to 1789, 6-8 million people were transported from the ports of the Lower Congo.[4] As the success of larger Congolese societies had become increasingly dependent on this lucrative trade, it comes as no surprise to learn that their downfall coincided with Britain's abolition of the slave trade in 1839 and its sinking of ships seen to be carrying human cargo. This was the case, at least, in western areas of the Congo. In the centre and east of the country the slave trade continued well into the 1890s with the Kazembe, Kuba and Lunda kingdoms growing powerful due to their business relations with Arab traders who had crossed the land from Khartoum in the Sudan or from Dar es Salaam in modern-day Tanzania. While large parts of the Kikongo kingdom would be integrated into northern Angola in the early 19th century, the gradual disappearance of the slave trade meant that its inhabitants had to find other means of making a living. Fortunately, other European nations seeking trading opportunities were to make their appearance in the Congo shortly after.

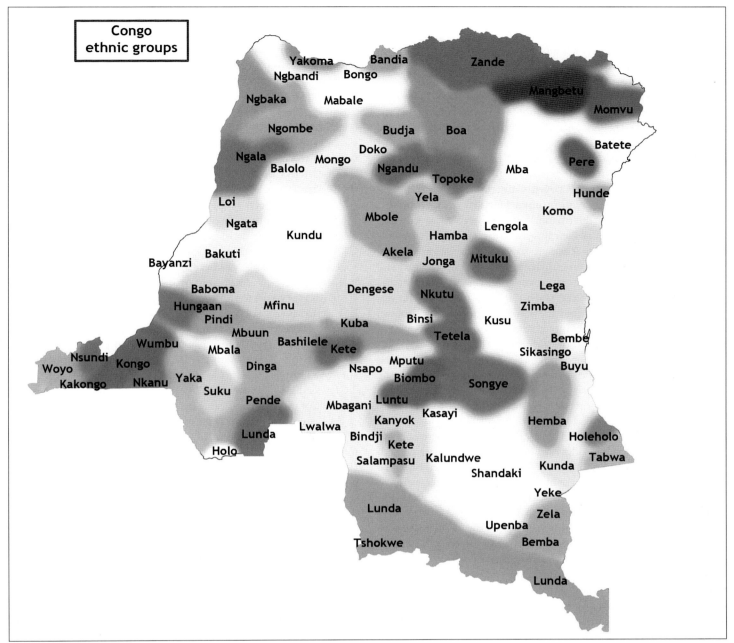

Ethnic groups in the Congo.

As geographical and botanical societies began to wonder what unknown lands and species lay beyond the coastal regions of the Congo, in 1816, the British admiralty gave Captain James Tuckey the mission of investigating whether there was a link between the Congo and Niger basins of western and central Africa. Though this mission aboard the aptly named HMS *Congo* ended when Tuckey and his crew died from fevers and attacks by natives, the publication of his notes in 1818 aroused much interest for wealthy individuals like Sir Joseph Banks, the President of the Royal Society who were prepared to sponsor further expeditions. A founder of the African Association, Banks is often credited as being one of the initiators of a period known as the age of African exploration.[5]

In other areas of research such as anthropology, Scottish missionaries led the way when it came to the study of African tribes and their traditions. Two names are of note: the Congregationalist missionary Robert Moffat and his son-in-law David Livingstone. Among the most celebrated explorers of the time, Moffat inspired Livingstone to explore the lands that lie to the north of Bechuanaland where no missionary had ever been. In 1854, under the service of the London Missionary Society (LMS) Livingstone embarked on a two-year-long voyage that would take him from Quelimane in Mozambique to Luanda in Angola. The first European to cross central Africa at that latitude, Livingstone discovered the existence of the Mosi-o-Tunya which he renamed Victoria Falls in honour of the British queen.

On the advice of fellow explorers, Richard Burton and John Hanning Speke, Livingstone then made further ground into the interior of the Congo and was able to explore the Kasai River and some of its tributaries. During subsequent expeditions, Livingstone discovered two other lakes in the Congo-Mweru and Bangweulu- and on his final expedition (1866-1873) he travelled up the Lualaba River also in search of the source of the Nile. Travelling to Ujiji in Tanganyika in 1871, it was here that Henry Morton Stanley uttered the immortal, 'Dr. Livingstone, I presume'.

In accounts of their respective voyages, these explorers related tales of the immense mineral riches which were to be found in south-eastern areas of the Congo such as Katanga.[6] With a history of mining dating back over 1,000 years,[7] the region was reputed all over central Africa for its source of copper long before the arrival of Europeans.[8] This metal was taken from the Katanga in the shape of St. Andrew's crosses, rings, axes, lances and different ornaments by Arab and black Portuguese traders and it was carried from the interior to the ports which lie on the shores of the Indian and Atlantic oceans. Indeed, in *The Last Journals* published in 1874, Livingstone was to describe how he came across a caravan of Arab traders near Lake Mweru[9] that was carrying more than five tons of copper such was its value. Other European explorers followed in Livingstone's footsteps. Englishman Verney Lovett Cameron; Scotland's Joseph Thomson – the geologist who inspired Haggard's *King Soloman's Mines* – and the German Hermann Wissman were all to mention traces of gold in accounts of their travels. The reports of Cameron's travels that appeared in *The Times* in early 1876 fascinated a public eager to know more about an enigmatic land, much of which still remained undiscovered. As well as catching the attention of the general public, the accounts also sparked interest in a man who was keen that Belgium should join the ranks of the major European nations and that it should acquire possessions abroad. The man in question was King Leopold II of Belgium.

To achieve his goal, in September 1876 Leopold invited around 40 explorers, scientists and philanthropists to his palace in the Belgian capital for what was to become the Brussels Geographic Conference. During this meeting, delegates decided to create the International African Association (IAA). Ostensibly, this association was the means through which Leopold could further altruistic and humanitarian projects by ridding this part of Central Africa of Arab slave traders. In practice, though, Leopold's regime turned out to be equally, if not more brutal and dehumanising. In effect, according to some estimates, Leopold's regime was responsible for the deaths of up to 10 million Congolese.[10]

Leopold's ambitions of empire in Africa began in 1879 when he funded an exploratory mission of the Congo Basin led by Sir Henry Morton Stanley. Over the next six years, Stanley would lead other missions of which the goal was to set up what would become the Congo Free State. Supposed to have been carried out in secrecy, Stanley's efforts were uncovered by the French who also held ambitions of extending their empire into the depths of the African continent. Pierre de Brazza was hastily dispatched to the western Congo basin and in 1881 was able to hoist the French flag above a settlement in modern-day Republic of the Congo named Brazzaville. Further penetration by the French took them into Guinea and across central Africa and Britain became worried that its trade routes through Egypt would be threatened if the French advance continued. Concurrently, both Italy and Germany were also making designs on establishing a presence in Ethiopia. This threatened to cut off British trade along the Nile. To solve potential dispute over boundaries that had not yet been drawn, diplomatic negotiations led to the Conference of Berlin which opened on 15 November 1884. Gathering representatives of 14 nations and ending on 26 February 1885, with the division of Africa completed according to the wants and needs of European powers, Leopold found himself in control of an area roughly 75 times larger than Belgium.

As Leopold's agents in the Free State set about securing the borders of what was in reality a trading zone, the true extent of the country's riches began to come to light. Based in the capital, Leopoldville, the city named by Stanley in honour of the Belgian king, employees of commercial enterprises such as Alexandre Delcommune of the Compagnie du Congo pour le Commerce et l'Industrie (CCCI), or military officers such as Lieutenant Paul Le Marinel made their way across the vast plains of Leopold's possession to cement claims in his name. Doing so meant that Le Marinel would often have to conclude treaties with the Congolese tribes he encountered. In 1891, Le Marinel made his way into Katanga in order to dissuade the British from laying claim to the areas around current-day northern Zambia. Through the establishment of another commercial concessionary organisation, the Company of Katanga (CK) or Compagnie du Katanga, and the drawing up of further treaties with native chiefs, in 1894 Leopold's sovereignty over the area in south-eastern Congo was cemented when the British acknowledged the border that separated Nyasaland and Katanga. With the border still not having been properly determined by 1900, Léopold and the Katanga Company again joined forces in order to create the Compagnie Spéciale de Katanga (Special Committee of the Katanga CSK). The mission of this concession was to carry out additional surveys of the Katanga's riches.[11]

Despite Belgian sovereignty over Katanga, British entrepreneur Cecil Rhodes was determined to gain a share of the riches contained in the province's subsoil. He and other British investors set up Tanganyika Concessions Limited (TCL) and negotiations carried out with the Katanga Company would eventually lead to the signing of a convention which granted TCL permission to carry out mining surveys. Through tests made on the soils around mines in Katanga, TCL was able to discover the richest deposits of copper in the world in terms of their size and value per ton of mineral extracted.[12]

As Leopold's barbaric reign over the Congo Free State drew to a close, a merger between TLC and the Katanga Company led, in 1906, to the creation of the Mining Union of Haut-Katanga (Union Minière du Haut-Katanga, UMHK). With finance being provided by the Société Générale de Belgique (SGB) and by private subscribers, the UMHK was awarded rights to exploit minerals in the region for 99 years.[13] In the following years when further geological reports showed the presence of copper in Katangan mines at Kambove, Kitulu, Kamaia, Kimbui and Kioabana, two more mining companies, the Société Forestière et Minière du Congo (Forminière) and the Compagnie du Chemin de Fer du Bas-Congo au Katanga (BCK) were awarded concessions by the Belgian government. As the need for technical expertise and labour continued to raise so did the number of Europeans who arrived in the province ready to claim a share in the prosperity.

In addition to the mainly Belgian immigration that took part at the turn of the century, the sheer size of Free State meant that the concessionary companies to which Leopold had sold trading rights relied heavily on the use of local labour to fully exploit the produce his possession had to offer. The terrain of the Congo varying greatly from region to region, the difficulties linked to the transportation of goods over long distances were overcome by the sometimes forced recruitment of the Congolese as carriers or porters. So significant was the amount of goods being transported out of the inner reaches of the Congo to its ports that from 1892 to 1898 the number of carriers increased from 40,000 to 2,730,533.[14]

Starting in 1890, the harvesting of rubber was the industry in which a majority of cutters and porters were used. Obtained from a species of vine named the Landolphia, rubber was a highly profitable commodity from which ventures such as the Anglo-Belgian India Rubber Company (ABIR) could make enormous profits. In one year, ABIR made a turnover of 100% of its initial stake,[15] with Leopold earning a profit of some 70 million Belgian francs purely through the exploitation of rubber.[16] Ivory was another profitable commodity for concessions such as the Compagnie Anversoise du

Promotional Poster for the Universal Exhibition in Brussels 1910. (via author)

Commerce au Congo and it was estimated that ivory valued at three and a half million francs was sold in Antwerp in the two years after the company was founded.[17]

To ensure that dissent from labourers was kept to a minimum and that the flow of valuable commodities could continue without hindrance, in 1885 Leopold established the Force Publique. With an officer corps recruited from Belgian, Scandinavian or Italian forces, the regular members of this unit was made up of an African soldiery recruited from warrior tribes from the Congo or from Nigerian Hausa tribesmen.[18] Under the auspices of British authorities, reinforcements were recruited from Liberia, the Gold Coast and Sierra Leone.[19] The role of the Force Publique was to ensure the internal security of the Free State and its first major military challenge came with the Congolese-Arab War (1892-1894). During this minor conflict, a Congolese ally of Arab slave traders named Gango Lutete of the Batetela tribe rebelled against the Free State. The execution of Lutete for treason by Free State authorities was to lead to the Batetela Rebellion in 1895 and two subsequent revolts in the next five years. These revolts took place at the garrison of Luluabourg in the Kasai; during an expedition led by Force Publique officer Francis Dhanis to the Upper Nile[20] and in 1900 at the Fort de Shinkakasa garrison near Boma, a port town in the west of the Congo and the capital of the Free State. To ward off further threats to the security of the Free State the number of recruits to the Force Publique increased to 20,000 by 1898 and it was reorganised so that no one ethnic group dominated its ranks.[21]

Other challenges to Leopold's sovereignty over the Free State came in the shape of reports in the UK and the USA of atrocities being committed against native groups residing in the Congo basin. The Aborigines' Protection Society (APS) of Great Britain pressured the British government to intervene and in 1903, it published Henry Richard Fox Bourne's *Civilisation in Congoland, a Story of International Wrong-Doing*.[22] This work told of how the Free State's agents would hold tribal chiefs prisoner until their people harvested the required amount of rubber; how women and children were beaten with the *chicotte* (a whip made from animal hide); and how villages were burnt to the ground when quotas were not met.[23] Other abuses of the Congolese population involved the construction of the railway that linked Matadi and Stanley Pool from 1890 to 1897. Of the thousands recruited by force, the rate of mortality for labourers working on the line reached 8.8% in 1892.[24]

As information on the abuses filtered out of the Free State, in 1903 the British government sent its Vice-Consul in the Congo, Roger Casement, to inspect conditions. His damning report published one year later, and further reports by British journalist Edmund Dene Morel in the same year led to the setting up of the Commission of Reforms to examine the role of Leopold's agents. Reform decrees were issued and at the end of 1907 and Leopold found himself obliged by the Belgian government to surrender his possessions in Central Africa. Through the ratification of the Colonial Charter, the Congo Free State became the Belgian Congo on 15 November 1908.

As was the case for many who left Europe for life in the colonies, the Belgians who set up home in the Congo attempted to recreate the society they had just left. Residing in fast-developing urban agglomerations such as Leopoldville, Stanleyville or Elisabethville, shop owners, bank managers, headmasters, and lawyers enjoyed the benefits of a colonial system whose officials were eager to promote the construction of churches, cinemas, restaurants, swimming pools and golf clubs. With the desire to bring 'civilisation' to central Africa, to build an empire in the heart of Africa, and to protect this way of life and ideology, the Belgian colonial administration continued to maintain the Force Publique. Composed of 160 European officers, 170 European non-commissioned officers, and 13,000 native Congolese in 1944, the number of recruits conscripted to serve in the force per annum was fixed at between 2,100 to 4,800. Officers and non-commissioned officers were seconded from the Belgian army while the native Congolese were recruited from different tribes. The Batetela, and the Bangala were particularly well represented. Larger urban areas such as Leopoldville, Stanleyville, Coquilhatville and Matadi also had a local law-enforcement officers serving in the police urbane.[25]

Social and economic progress in the Belgian Congo

Though sometimes barbaric methods were employed during Léopold II's tenancy of the Congo Free State, social and economic programmes designed by Belgian authorities from the 1920s set the foundations for the modernisation of the Congo. The realisation that the Congo possessed such an abundance of mineral resources drew thousands of Belgians and other Europeans to the Congo in the years before the Great War. In terms of developing an infrastructure adapted to transport minerals to the exterior, however, the Belgian Congo only truly began to emerge as an economic powerhouse in the 1920s. This was due to a programme of reform implemented by Louis Frank of the Colonial Office. Frank's plan to restructure the Congo was drawn along two axes: one that would deal with economic aspects and the other with social aspects. Although the Compagnie du Chemin de Fer du Congo (CCFC) had completed a functioning network of rail links by 1898, Frank had the vision of extending this network into the far reaches of the Congo in order to 'spread civilisation and to exploit the economic opportunities

Promotional Poster for Sabena Airlines. (via author)

that the Congo had to offer'.[26] Not a supporter of fully state-owned enterprises, the plan was to partially privatise the network to encourage investment. The railway system was not the only economic infrastructure concerned by the reforms: Frank wanted to revitalise the Congo's ports, make Katangan mines more productive, and provide the means for the province's copper to be transported across the Kasai to the Atlantic Ocean. Waterways were equally important to economic development. Organised river transport had begun as early as 1881 with the Marine du Haut Congo operating steamers, and in 1925 this company merged with the Union Nationale des Transports Fluviaux (UNATRA). Over the coming years, the union was absorbed by the Office d'Exploitation des Transports Coloniaux (OTRACO). One of the pioneers of aviation in Africa, by 1920 a link had been established between Leopoldville and Stanleyville by the Société Nationale pour l'Etude des Transports Aériens (SNETA),[27] and this study into the possibilities offered by transport by air led to the founding of the Société Anonyme Belge d'Exploitation de la Navigation Aérienne (SABENA) in 1923. Sabena operated flights between the Congo and Europe.[28]

On the question of social reforms, improving the Congo's agricultural and farming landscapes was another area that drew Frank's attention. This, he said, would enable the indigenous population to have access to more abundant and better quality food. The growing of cotton was another option that Frank would put forward to government ministers. In his opinion, if a colony was to be successful it needed private companies that would provide specialist expertise. For this reason, Frank called upon the Special Committee of the Katanga and Forminière. As well as owning lands destined for the mining sector, both held large tracts of land reserved for agricultural exploitation. Cotonco was yet another company seen as important in Frank's plans. The objective of reforming the Congo's socio-economic backdrop required a substantial increase in the number of qualified and unqualified workers. In addition to providing subsidies and bonuses to all sections of the Belgian population willing to come to the Congo, improving the lives of the country's native population also became a priority. This would be achieved by increasing the number of educational and medical facilities, and Belgian teachers and doctors were, therefore, also encouraged to move to the colony. When it came to the question of who would perform which duties in this restructured economy, due to its 'current level of knowledge and its capabilities', according to Frank, the role of the indigenous population was to work in 'technical' areas of industry. Those who were deemed as particularly intelligent could eventually become clerks or even medical assistants.[29]

Though Frank's comments can be interpreted as symptomatic of a form of ingrained racism, the concept of 'equality' between blacks and whites was virtually unknown. Rather, Belgian authorities believed that if they were reaping the economic benefits of the exploitation of natural resources, they also had the duty of improving the lives of Africans. They should be taken from a society based on tribal rituals towards one based on Christianity and on a western belief system. This paternalist approach is illustrated by the reforming of the Congolese educational system initiated in 1922. Primary education, it was thought, would more likely

Congolese *évolués*, colonial subjects that had adopted a measure of the European lifestyle. (courtesy: researchgate.net)

ensure a contented population and the introduction of secondary education would give the Congolese the possibility to work as nurses, mechanics, etc. From the mid-1920s, the state encouraged an increase in the number schools and put particular emphasis on religious education. In 1941, there were six state schools for the native Congolese; three state schools for Europeans; and over 5,200 mission schools for the native Congolese. Mission schools also existed for European children. Run by the Christian Brothers, the Marist Brothers and Salesian Fathers, the English Baptist Missionary, these schools prepared students for technical schools operated by UMHK or by Lever.[30] Authorities were equally aware of the need to educate future tribal chiefs and set up a school in Buta in northern Congo. While there was no provision for the Congolese to enter the liberal professions or to attend university at that time, a series of reforms carried out in the 1920s and, again in the 1930s, saw the emergence of middle-class Congolese elite holding jobs that were relatively well paid.

With the Belgian Congo already possessing the highest developed educational system in tropical Africa by 1958 – the number of primary school pupils outstripping similar systems in British West Africa, British East Africa and French colonies on the continent[31] – investment in the economic infrastructure of the Congo was also a priority for post-Second World War governments. In 1950, Belgium embarked on a Ten Year Plan which would see £45 million spent on roads, around £104 million spent on river, lake, rail and air communications, more than £21 million on providing power, £16 million on improving water supplies, and £54 million on improving housing for civil servants, some of whom were Congolese.[32] The results of the investment were seen very rapidly as far as industrial production was concerned. By 1953, for example, the Congo had become Africa's leading producer of cobalt, tin, diamonds, zinc, silver and tungsten while, after Northern Rhodesia, it was the second largest producer of copper. Africans also benefitted greatly. Their share in the national income increased from 46% in 1950 to 58% in 1958[33] and average income for the Congolese was higher than many other African countries: in 1955 annual income per person in the Congo was estimated at £27[34] while it was £22 in Nigeria; £21 in Kenya; and £20 in Uganda.[35] As incomes increased, so did the desire to enjoy a western lifestyle: the Congolese began to purchase electrical goods, textiles, alcohol, and even cars. On top of these developments in terms of salaries, the Congolese also benefitted from family allowances, illness and accident insurance and pensions. As far as the latter is concerned, a decree issued on 6 June 1956 made the Belgian Congo the first colonial power to institute pensions for native employees in private enterprises in sub-Saharan Africa.[36]

Another area where vast improvements were made in the 1950s in the Congo is that of race relations. Whereas South Africa and some southern US states still enforced by law what is known informally as the 'colour bar', in the Belgian Congo there was no official government policy implementing separation along racial lines. In fact, if there was segregation, it appears that this was a matter of convention: inter-racial marriage and social intercourse were not prohibited; there were no laws excluding the Congolese from employment in certain sectors to perform certain roles; and there was no attempt by trade unions to discriminate against Congolese workers. If more whites than blacks were found in higher-paid jobs carrying a greater degree of social prestige, it was primarily because they enjoyed a better level of education.[37]

So if throughout the 1950s the lives of the Congolese had improved so much and, on paper, they had as much chance of benefitting from the colonial system as the Belgians, the question begs as to why there was such a profound desire on behalf of the Congolese for independence. It could be that it had taken half a century for the Belgians to provide some level of equality to the Congolese; it could be that an international context of decolonisation was fermenting desires to imitate countries such as Ghana or the neighbouring French Congo; and it could be that the benefits of social and economic development enjoyed by the white population and the educated Congolese was not available to the vast majority of Congolese, especially those living in rural areas such as the Kwilu. Virtually unarmed politically and increasingly isolated from the social and political advances being made in urban areas, this rural population was beleaguered to pay taxes to support the demands of a system from which it did not, and could not, fully benefit. If all the factors above certainly did make a contribution to promoting wishes for independence, there is one overriding aspect that generated consequences undoubtedly not envisaged by the reformers who sought to modernise the Congo and the colonial system. By providing education, by providing equal opportunities, and by providing the means to formulate ideologies, Belgium had unwittingly and inadvertently given the Congolese the nous with which it could do political battle. Similarly to the fruit that the Kwilu's cutters harvested to eke out a living, a relic of Leopold II's oppression, the Congolese were ripe. Ripe for rebellion.

2
Congolese Political Development, 1946–1959

There are a number of examples that demonstrate the Congolese willingness to react violently when the authorities seemingly abused their powers and made exaggerated demands or forcefully imposed rigid colonial doctrines. This was the case during the Batetela Rebellion in 1895 and, even in a context of social and economic reform, this was the case when the Pende revolted in 1931. In June of that year, when territorial agent Edouard Burnotte turned up in the Kwilu to forcefully recruit men for the plantations and to demand taxes, he was cut up into pieces by Pénde tribesmen and his body parts were subsequently distributed to village elders.[1]

Though this peasant revolt was repressed by the Force Publique – a repression which led to the death of more than 500 native Congolese – anger and resentment were never far from the surface. These emotions were not limited to rural areas and they were to resurface just over a decade later, this time in Katanga. Unhappy at not being allowed to set up associations of a political nature but wanting to protest against pay and working conditions, in January 1942, black miners at Jadotville and Elisabethville initiated a strike over pay and racial segregation in the mines. Refusing an offer of a 30% increase during negotiations at a local stadium in Elisabethville, the governor general of the province, Amour Maron ordered his troops to open fire. Estimates put the number of deaths between 30 and 70.² Next, in December 1943, *évolués* attempted to gain support from Congolese soldiers for another strike, this time in Luluabourg in the Kasai, but on New Year's Eve were informed by these soldiers of the Force Publique that they were planning a mutiny. If the *évolués* chose to join them the movement could gain national support. Led by Sergeant-Major Ngoie Mukalabushi, a mutiny began in February 1944. After attacking the camp's arsenal, mutineers then ransacked houses in white areas, destroyed symbols of colonial rule and declared their wishes for independence of the Congo. Two mutineers including Mukalabushi were arrested and shot.³ Acts of protest also occurred in the Lower Congo from 15 September to the end of December 1945. Several people were killed in riots on 26-27 November in Matadi.⁴

Being prohibited by law from forming political alliances, the Congolese were, nevertheless, actively encouraged to join associations of a cultural and tribal nature. No doubt having some relation to the divide and rule policies of the British in India, the creation of these associations was to lead to the development of a political awakening in the Congo. Among early examples of this type of association are the Fédération Kasaienne set up in Leopoldville (Kinshasa) in 1916; the Fédération Kwangolaise set up in 1925; and other ethnic associations which were established in Katanga as early as 1926.[5] Another source of affiliation which developed political enlightenment was the educational reforms implemented in the 1920s. This allowed for the alumni of mission schools such as the Association des Anciens Elèves des Pères de Scheut (ADAPES) to set up old boy networks.[6]

In addition to these home-grown associations, the advent and spread of black political activism in the United States and Europe finally reached the Congo in 1946 when Eslanda Goode Robeson visited Leopoldville during a tour of African countries. The wife of singer and actor Paul Robeson, Eslanda Robeson met Congolese intellectuals such as Joseph Kasa-Vubu in Leopoldville in 1946.[7] She shared her husband's ideology of advocating and promoting black cultural nationalism, or Pan-Africanism, and she linked the liberation struggles of blacks in her American homeland to those in Africa. Paul Robeson had also created the Council of African Affairs believing, deeply, that 'self-sustained and self-propelled black movements [were] the only effective strategy to combat the imperialist psychological propaganda of cultural degradation'.[8] Another step in the Congo's political awakening occurred in 1946 just after the work-related riots of the previous year. Indeed, though indigenous labour unions continued to be proscribed, a change in the Congo's industrial landscape was to be achieved through the establishment of the Association du Personnel Indigène du Congo Belge et du Ruanda-Urundi (APIC).[9]

Following his meetings with Eslanda Robeson, Joseph Kasa-Vubu would be at the forefront of the movement to bring about meaningful political change in the Congo. Educated at Catholic missions and employed as a clerk in the Finance Department of the Governor-General's office, it was after having honed his political ideology as a member of the Union des Intérêts Sociaux Congolais (UNISCO) that, in 1955, Kasa-Vubu became chairman of the Alliance des Bakongo (ABAKO). Created in 1950 by Edmond Nzaza-Landu, and starting life as a cultural association of Kikongo-speaking Congolese, the ABAKO would soon develop into the most influential driving force behind obtaining independence for the Congo.[10] After its creation and after it had received official recognition from the Belgian authorities, the ABAKO sought to spread an influence which had to that point been limited to geographical areas where there were the highest concentrations of Bakongo tribesmen. Between 1951 and 1953, the ABAKO extended its areas of activity from Leopoldville to Matadi and Thysville. This was done in order to establish links with co-operatives, youth groups and student associations.[11]

Continuing with this strategy of setting up localised political connections over the next three years, the ABAKO was thrown into the arena of national politics in 1956 after a report by Belgian academic Anton Arnold Van Bilsen suggested that the Congo could achieve independence following a 30-year transitional period.[12] Conciliatory in tone and content, Van Bilsen criticised Belgium's 'half-century domination' of the Congo, its 'outmoded methods', and its failure to train doctors, veterinarians, and engineers. In his view, the period of political emancipation of the Congo [was] opening and that Congolese independence was 'inevitable'.[13] Though a group of Catholic Africans including Joseph Ileo mirrored Van Bilsen's comments in a manifesto published in July 1956 in *Conscience Africaine*, their comments were vague in nature insofar as the role Belgian political parties would play in the emancipation programme.[14] The manifesto stated political institutions in the Belgian Congo would undergo progressive change, and a nominative system would be replaced by one which saw the Congolese elect its own representatives. Moreover, Congolese advisory bodies which currently performed a purely consultative role would receive more authority in decision-making so that they would be ready to form a government when the time came. It also argued against the creation of political parties in the Congo seeing them as 'a useless evil' due to their different political objectives. What were needed at this time, according to Ileo, were union and not division.[15] Although this manifesto was the first demonstration of the Congolese desire to determine their own future, Ileo's thoughts were highly criticised in a 'Counter-Manifesto' published by ABAKO in August 1956. As evidence of division within the ABAKO camp and differences between Ileo and Kasa-Vubu, it rejected out of hand the idea that Belgium should help shape the Congo. Stating that Van Bilsen's plan should be 'annihilated' as it would only retard Congolese independence further, this manifesto saw the differing objectives of political parties as 'dangerous but necessary in a democracy'.[16] Instead, and reflecting its own ideology, it put forward the suggestion that groups which were linked historically, ethnically and linguistically should be part of a Congolese Federation.[17]

By the time the political future of the Congo had started to swing in favour of the Congolese, events taking place in the international arena were to have a substantial influence on the evolution of the question of independence. While pressure was put on colonising nations to promote the concepts of equal rights and self-determination for non self-governing territories, perhaps the most significant boost to national and political awareness in the Congo was the rise in popularity of Pan-Africanism. Since its creation in 1900, the influence of a movement founded by Trinidadian lawyer Henry Sylvester Williams reached the shores of the African continent via Kwame Nkrumah. After studying in the United States and Britain where he had honed his political philosophy, in 1945 Nkrumah co-hosted the Fifth Pan-African Congress which was held in Manchester from 15-21 October. Attended by 90 delegates, with 26 from Africa, the objective of the congress was to discuss the issues facing a large part of the African continent in respect of the remits of the UN charter. After one week of talks, it was resolved that imperialism and the monopolisation of 'private wealth and industry for profit alone' should be condemned, and that every option was open when it came to the question of achieving political and economic independence.¹⁸

Looking on as Ghana became the first sub-Saharan African nation to reach these goals was Patrice Emery Lumumba. Born into the humble surroundings of Onalua in the Kasai province in 1925, Lumumba belonged to the Batetela ethnic group, known for its resistance to Belgian colonial authority. Although, Lumumba was not a gifted child from an intellectual point of view, his assertive temperament and his refusal to accept the authority of the teachers saw him expelled from Methodist and Catholic missionary schools. In 1944 Lumumba moved to Stanleyville in the Congo's Eastern Province where he obtained work as a postal clerk in the civil service. Shortly after, Lumumba began to take an interest in Congolese affairs and in 1952 he joined the Association des évolués de Stanleyville and the Batetela de Léopoldville. In each case, he furthered his political ambitions by transforming these socio-cultural associations into political groups by opposing the majority of the often docile members.¹⁹ Committed to improving race relations and a supporter of the creation of the Belgo-Congolese community expounded by *Conscience Africaine*, in 1956 Lumumba was invited to Brussels to meet King Baudouin. Considered as a potential ministerial advisor, Lumumba's political career came to a brief halt that same year when he was imprisoned for allegedly having misappropriated public funds. By the time Lumumba was released some 14 months later, his political ideology had changed from being supportive of a transitional period to wanting independence for the Congo as soon as possible. Identifying his own struggles with authority to the struggles faced by the Congolese as a nation,²⁰ on 5 October 1958 Lumumba joined the burgeoning Mouvement National Congolais (MNC).

Lumumba's rapid emergence as a force in nationalist politics was recognised almost immediately by some of Africa's most radical leaders when – to replace Kasa-Vubu as the Congolese delegate – he was invited to attend the First All-African People's Conference held in Accra, Ghana in December 1958. The conference brought together 300 delegates representing 65 organisations from 28 African countries, and strong representation came from North African countries which had obtained, or were in the process of obtaining, independence. West, east and central African countries all had significant delegations as did the United States.²¹ Its delegates included Eslanda Robeson and Shirley Graham Du Bois, the wife of W.E.B. Du Bois, the Pan-Africanist founder of the National Association for the Advancement of Coloured People (NAACP) in 1909.

When the time came for Lumumba to address the delegates, he demonstrated exactly why he was held in such high esteem. Considering the founding of the MNC as 'a decisive step for the Congolese people as they move toward emancipation' in respect of the Universal Declaration of the Rights of Man and UN Charter, the MNC wished to 'create a modern democratic state' which would grant its citizens 'freedom, justice, social peace, tolerance, well-being and equality with no discrimination whatsoever'.²² Verbally attacking the 'injustices' and the 'stupid superiority complex'²³ of the colonists, Lumumba's message must have been music to the ears of other Pan-Africanists such as Nkrumah, Kenneth Kaunda and Hastings Banda. Despite ethnic differences and the boundaries that separated African nations, all had the 'same awareness', the same 'anguished soul', and the same 'anxious desire' to free the African continent of fear and of colonist domination.²⁴ Foreshadowing the problems which lay ahead, however, Lumumba also warned that the factitious nature of a Congolese nation divided along tribal

Patrice Lumumba during one of his many pre-independence public appearances.

and religious lines was a serious hindrance to what he described as the 'flowering of a harmonious and fraternal African society'.²⁵ For a man with little academic training, Lumumba's own political awareness and his ability to analyse the divisive nature of Congolese society and politics were unerringly accurate: discordant opinions had been voiced in reaction to the manifestos issued by *Conscience Africaine* and the ABAKO, and two new political parties – the Centre de regroupement african (CEREA) in North Kivu, and the Conféderation des associations tribales du Katanga (CONAKAT) – had just been created. Both were tribal and both represented the interests of regional populations.²⁶

Taking advantage from the MNC being seen as the only political representative of the nation as a whole and taking on the role of a government-in-waiting, two weeks after the Accra Conference, Lumumba organised a meeting of MNC supporters in Leopoldville. Through a denunciation of Belgium's policy of divide and rule in the Congo, Lumumba now confirmed that he possessed the characteristics and the vision that were needed to lead that very same government. Also showing that he was ready to fulfil this role was Joseph Kasa-Vubu. His party having won a majority of seats in the municipal elections held in December 1957 – the first elections in which the Congolese were allowed to participate – in January 1959 Kasa-Vubu also convened a meeting of his supporters which was due to be held at the Young Men's Christian Association headquarters in Leopoldville. Warned by Belgian officials that if the meeting became political Kasa-Vubu would be held responsible and gaining the impression that the meeting was banned, on 3 January Kasa-Vubu then attempted to postpone the meeting. Despite these attempts a large crowd of supporters from the Bakongo tribe gathered in front of the YMCA where further appeals from Kasa-Vubu failed to disperse them.²⁷ Rioting then broke out and the subsequent burning of cars and businesses, and attacks on whites and members of other tribes resulted in a death toll of somewhere between 49 and 500.²⁸ After the riots, Kasa-Vubu and two other ABAKO leaders were arrested and sent to Belgium for trial. This only exacerbated racial tensions in the Congo.²⁹ Later that year, in October, a meeting organised by Lumumba in Stanleyville (Kisangani) also left 70 people dead. As was the case with Kasa-Vubu, Lumumba was also arrested by security police.³⁰ The nature of the riots in Leopoldville

Rioters at the Fina Petrol Station, Leopoldville, January 1959.

Rioters armed with a few old rifles, and bows and arrows on the streets of Leopoldville, in July 1960.

Belgian troops deployed during Operation Mangrove, July 1960.

also announced that it would accompany the Congolese through a transitional period during which Congolese officials would be able to participate in executive and legislative procedures. Racial discrimination was to be abolished and there was to be an Africanisation of the administration.[31]

With political parties jostling for position in what was becoming a context characterised by inter-tribal dispute the Luluabourg Congress was organised in April 1959 where it was hoped that tribal electoral lists would be prohibited.[32] As rivalries continued throughout 1959, in December Baudouin made his first visit to the colony since 1955. While many observers admired the courage of the young monarch, others reacted with surprise and believed that the visit constituted a last throw of the dice in the effort to ease tensions between coloniser and colonised. A second congress between representatives of different Congolese parties was held in Bukavu in eastern Congo between 6-8 January 1960 and the peaceful atmosphere of the meetings held between these dates set the stage for the talks between Belgian and Congolese that took place in Brussels between 20 January-20 February 1960. A second series of meetings took place from 26 April-16 May of the same year. It was in Brussels that the political and tribal rivalries that had led to so much division in the Congo from 1958 started to reappear. These divisions even included a split inside the MNC when, following disagreement between Lumumba and Albert Kalonji the latter created the Mouvement National Congolais-Kalonji (MNC-K). This had come about after Lumumba had lent support to the Lulua people in the Kasai region of the Congo. A Baluba, Kalonji opposed any measure that would give an advantage to a bitter enemy such as the Lulua. Along with ABAKO and the Parti Solidaire Africain (PSA), or

and an atmosphere within which whites were becoming increasingly threatened with violence moved King Baudouin to make a speech on 13 January 1959 in which he recognised the rights of the Congolese to self-determination. On the same day, the Belgian government

African Solidarity Party, Kalonji opposed Lumumba's concept of a unitary state governed from Léopoldville and, instead, argued that the Congo should be a loose federation of separate states.³³ In spite of the differences in opinion, participants at the Conference nevertheless agreed that independence should be set for 30 June 1960 and that provincial and legislative elections should be held a month earlier.

In an endorsement of his popularity in the Orientale, Kivu and Kasai provinces, Patrice Lumumba was to emerge triumphant in these elections. Obtaining 33 of a possible 137 seats available, and well ahead of Kasa-Vubu and Kalonji, Lumumba now found himself the most influential and powerful man in Congolese politics. While news of the returns in the elections brought joy to Lumumba's supporters, for Europeans in the Congo the results cemented pre-election fears that they would become the target of anti-colonial sentiment. Indeed, in Lumumba's stronghold of Stanleyville, some Europeans were insulted and stoned, leading them to describe the leader of the MNC as 'most dangerous'.³⁴ In other parts of the Congo, after similar scenes took place, many Europeans were reported to be sending their wives and children away from the Congo after lists of Europeans and their residences were published in African newspapers. Allegedly, this was even the case in Katanga, a province hostile to Lumumba.³⁵ Sharing the opinion that Lumumba in a position of power was dangerous, and believing that Lumumba would seek to impose himself on Congolese Cabinet affairs, the Belgian officials sent to oversee the transition from colony to independence were nevertheless wary of attempting to exclude Lumumba from any government formed through the provisions of the recently drawn up constitution.³⁶

A scene from a street in Leopoldville, much of which was damaged during the ANC mutiny. A patrol of Belgian troops supported by two M8 armoured scout cars can be seen.

Voting Tendencies during the Congo elections of May 1960. (Young, 1968)

This type of political manoeuvring continued throughout June 1960 with, on the one hand, Lumumba attempting to form a government and, on the other, Joseph Kasa-Vubu talking of establishing a separate Mukongo province. Moïse Tshombe of Katanga also threatened to secede immediately if an amendment giving the province greater representation in the Congolese parliament was not added to the draft constitution.³⁷ In turn, in north-eastern Katanga, Jason Sendwe of the Association Générale des Baluba de Katanga (BALUBAKAT) was also declaring its determination to set up a separate state, one that would act in opposition to Tshombe's Conakat.³⁸ Here, the political situation

Belgian troops securing the docks of the port of Matadi, in July 1960.

Moise Tshombe (centre) and Albert Kalonji (right), in front of a USAF C-130.

worsened when tribal conflict between the Lulua and Baluba tribes led to a state of emergency being declared on 14 June. Further political wrangling continued over the next few days as political rivals jockeyed for position in the Congo's upper and lower houses. This included Lumumba opponent Joseph Ileo being elected head of the Congolese Senate over the Lumumba-supported Alexandre Mahamba. Despite opposition to his own candidates, in a sign of magnanimity Lumumba continued in his efforts to form a broadly based Cabinet that included rivals. Lumumba, whose party had gained control over the House of Representatives, was then invited by Walter Van der Meersh to form a government. Political compromise was reached through the composition of Lumumba's first Cabinet. On 23 June, with Lumumba holding the dual role of Prime Minister and Defence Minister, concessions were made to Conakat by putting this party in charge of the Ministry of Economics. As for other appointments, Lumumbists Justin Bomboko became Foreign Minister and Thomas Kanza was named as the Congo's United Nations delegate. The composition of the Congo's first government was completed with the election of Joseph Kasa-Vubu as Head of State on 24 June and to all appearances the country could now look forward to officially gaining its independence less than a week later. Below this surface of optimism though lay simmering tensions that were soon to throw the Congo into chaos.

Refusing to accept that the Congo had fallen into the hands of extremists wishing to impose a unitary structure over the country and having seen Balubakat political rival Jason Sendwe appointed State Commissioner for the province, Moïse Tshombe flew back to Elisabethville on 23 June. The same day, Tshombe declared that he was withdrawing his support for Lumumba.[39] With fears that Katanga would secede, on 28 June, Lumumba had met with Force Publique chief Lieutenant General Janssens and, in the scope of Article 250 of an agreement put in place between Congo and Belgian governments,[40] it was decided that Katanga would be brought into the union through force if necessary.[41] Secondly, during an impromptu speech given by Lumumba in the Palais de la Nation on Independence Day itself, Lumumba launched into a violent denunciation of Belgian rule in front of representatives from Asian and African countries as well as the world's press. For some, this was when 'trouble started', and the Crisis began.[42]

3
From Independence to Crisis

On 30 June 1960, as King Baudouin's official cortege made its way through the capital city named in honour of his great uncle Leopold II, he was greeted by thousands of Congolese who lined the streets which would lead him to the Palais de la Nation where he would put an end to just over 50 years of Belgian rule. For security forces protecting Baudouin's open-topped limousine, it appeared at one point that not all of the spectators had peaceful intentions: a smartly dressed man dashed from the crowd and drew the King's ceremonial sword from its scabbard. Though many feared for the King's life, the assailant simply danced alongside the car in a demonstration of celebration. Some observers remarked that the seizing of the sword symbolised the transfer of colonial power to a native African power.[1] The euphoria shown by the crowds was short-lived and a far more controversial sign that the Congolese had seized national authority came in the form of the speeches given to the international dignitaries who congregated in the palace situated on the banks of the River Congo. Baudouin was one of the first to rise and spoke of how the independence of the Congo was the culmination of work carried out by Leopold. This work included delivering the Congo basin from slavery; giving the Congo's different ethnic groups a national identity and leaving the Congolese with a moral and material heritage. For this, stated Baudouin, the Congolese should be grateful.

This reminder of the past came as a shock for many Congolese who thought it inappropriate that they be lectured by someone who no longer had authority over the country. Indeed, it seemed that Baudouin had misjudged the atmosphere in a building which had once served as the residence of the Governor General.[2] After a speech by President Joseph Kasa-Vubu, Lumumba prepared himself for a reply and rose from his place alongside Belgian Premier Gaston Eyskens. Displaying Belgium's highest decoration, the Order of the Crown, an award that he had been given the night before the ceremony, Lumumba gave his own version of Belgian colonial rule. Instead of the illustrious work described by Baudouin, Lumumba spoke of how the Congolese had been involved in a 'day-to-day fight', a fight 'to put an end to the humiliating slavery' which had been imposed by force.[3] Whereas Lumumba was to go some way in repairing relations with a toast to Belgian rule at a dinner given after the ceremony of independence, Lumumbists such as Placide Kitungwe, a member of Lumumba's first cabinet, believed that the speech was exactly what the Congolese wanted to hear.[4] Many also believed that Lumumba had

Enthusiasm for independence of the Congo of 1960 led some women to dress themselves for the occasion.

King Baudouin and Joseph Kasa-Vubu are taken to the Palais de la Nation, Leopoldville, 30 June 1960.

Joseph Kasa-Vubu, Patrice Lumumba and King Baudouin of Belgium, 30 June 1960.

An image of the scene that symbolised the transfer of power from the Belgians to the Congolese, as King Baudouin's ceremonial sword was taken away by a Congolese man while the ceremonial car travelled through the streets of Leopoldville, 30 June 1960.

commander General Emile Janssens at Camp Léopold II in Léopoldville on 5 July were dismayed to learn that, as far as they were concerned, nothing had changed. Janssens illustrated this rather bluntly by writing "before Independence equals after Independence" on a blackboard. The NCOs were even more disconcerted to learn that Lumumba had asked white officers to remain and that they would be appointed to key positions within the Congo security forces. Though Lumumba attempted to negotiate peace with the NCOs, his leaving the meeting accompanied by Janssens only served to stoke anger. The NCOs attacked other white officers at the camp, tried to force their way into parliament, and threatened to open fire. Two days later, with Lumumba still not giving in to their demands, and with the soldiers now laying siege outside his official residence, Lumumba found himself obliged to backtrack on his previous announcements. Dismissing Janssens and all his white officers, Lumumba then declared his intention to Africanise the Congo's security forces and to promote each NCO.[7] He then replaced Janssens with his ageing uncle Victor Lundula as commander-in-chief of the newly-created Congolese National Army (Armée Nationale Congolais, ANC). Joseph-Désiré Mobutu was appointed chief of staff while the Belgian officer Colonel Henniquian became the ANC's military advisor. As we shall see, Lumumba's naming of Mobutu was an act of political naivety that would cost him dear. In effect, by the refusal to listen to apparently well-founded rumours of Mobutu's links to Belgian and American intelligence services, Lumumba had unwittingly chosen his own Judas.[8]

Lumumba's moves did little to calm the ardour and anger of the ANC mutineers and after the homes and businesses of Europeans had been ransacked in Leopoldville, it was the turn of other larger cities such as Matadi and the military base at Camp Hardy. Spreading east, the mutiny reached Kongolo in northern Katanga and Camp Massart in Elisabethville. The riots which included the gang-raping of women and children as young as 12 forced thousands of Europeans to seek refuge.[9] Many left the Congo by road or rail, fled to neighbouring Angola, or crossed the River Congo into Brazzaville. In Northern Rhodesia, there was talk of forming units of commandos to rescue Europeans fleeing Elisabethville.

overstepped the mark and that the speech had been unnecessarily inflammatory.

Despite celebrations being slightly soured by the content of these verbal disagreements, neither the Belgian nor the Congolese authorities wished to see a disorganised handover of power. Moreover, both sides demonstrated their willingness to provide the basis for a programme of mutual aid through the Treaty of Friendship, Assistance and Cooperation signed on Independence Day.[5] Over the next four days the Congolese cities and countryside remained largely trouble-free with the Congo's European population of 29,000 being protected by just over 1,000 Belgian officers and 23,000 non-commissioned Congolese who formed the Force Publique.[6] But while a spirit of cooperation existed in administrative circles and both Belgian and Congolese worked hand-in-hand to achieve a peaceful transition, it was within the Force Publique that, paradoxically, there was the most discord. Expecting to see their salaries increased, and expecting to be promoted with the departure of their white officers, the NCOs gathered before their

Congolese civilians in nearby Kabalo were also complicit in the mutiny: some attempted to stop the departure of a train to Elisabethville carrying 250 Europeans to safety and they joined riots which took place in the mining towns of Shinkolobwe and Kolwezi.[10] Another caught up in the chaos was CIA Chief of Station, Larry Devlin. Arriving in Leopoldville on 10 July, he was mistaken for a Belgian and taken prisoner. Made to kiss the boots of his captors, Devlin had been threatened with death.[11] In all, 26,000 Europeans left the Congo before the 10 July.[12] The reports of the killing and raping of its citizens brought a stern response from the Belgian government, and when six Europeans were killed in Katanga around 800 Belgian paratroopers and commandos were flown into Elisabethville on 10 July where they fought against the ANC mutineers. Belgium also launched Operation Mangrove in which its warships bombarded the port of Matadi and warplanes from the Kitona military base attacked mutineers.[13] This intervention brought an end to the entente between the Congo and Belgium, the former severing all diplomatic ties.

Moise Tshombe greeting supporters in Katanga.

It was inevitable that these large-scale, widespread and sometimes violent disturbances would lead to the type of repercussion exercised so succinctly by Belgium. Similar demonstrations of political and military protest at the deterioration of the context were to follow very shortly, and a series of secessions and declarations of independence saw a unitary state splinter into several smaller units almost all with their own political agenda. On occasions, the desire for self-determination of opposing ethnic groups was determinant in producing a split within a split, as we shall see in the case of Katanga. This, however, will be examined in the following chapter when the secession of this province will be discussed in greater detail. For the moment, suffice it to say that with reports that transport, postal services and lines of communication were now being severely disrupted, Tshombe's weapon of choice used to express his dissatisfaction with the anarchic situation of the Congo was to declare that Katanga had decided to follow its own path from 11 July. Evidently, due to Katanga's mineral riches and its providing the Congolese government with a very large percentage of its revenues, Tshombe's declaration came as a massive blow for Lumumba. Faced with the task of implementing social reform but, all the while, requiring economic prosperity in order to do so, Lumumba had lost the Congo's greatest financial asset. Worse still, his lacking the experience of a statesman and affected by geopolitical naivety Lumumba would then make a series of disastrous decisions. Ultimately, they would lead to his downfall and to his complete elimination from the Congolese political arena.

After failing to quell the rioting and failing to obtain a diplomatic solution to the Katanga question through negotiations with Tshombe – the Katangese leader refusing permission for the aircraft carrying Lumumba to land[14] – Lumumba's first mistake was to break diplomatic relations with Belgium, the only country capable

Tshombe and Godefroid Munongo at the declaration of Katangan Independence, 11 July 1960.

of providing the prime minister with the political leverage needed in any future negotiations with Tshombe. Then, seemingly unaware that his actions would exacerbate already delicate East-West relations, Lumumba's next mistake was to call on the Union of Soviet Socialist Republics (USSR) for assistance in removing Belgian military forces.[15] Thankfully, by 13/14 July, the UN was in the process of weighing up the pros and cons of the so-called Tunisian Resolution whereby the organisation's Security Council would call upon Belgium to withdraw its troops and authorise its Secretary-General to take the necessary measures to do so. Assistance, provided through the United Nations Operations in the Congo (UNOC), would be given until Congolese national security forces were in a position to maintain order.[16] What the UN, itself, failed to understand at the time is that the inclusion of this condition was unrealistic in view

One of about a dozen Ilyushin Il-14 transports, donated by Moscow to the Congolese government in 1960: their presence helped construct the notion that Lumumba was pro-USSR.

Indian Army Daimler armoured cars as seen on arrival in the Congo, July 1960.

of the shambolic state of the ANC. Still, on 15 July, UN Resolution 143 resulted in the arrival of the first of 20,000 peacekeepers in the Congo. By 25 July, 8,000 Tunisian, Moroccan, Swedish, Liberian, Irish, Ethiopian, Guinean and Ghanaian peacekeepers had been assigned to the mission and by 31 July they numbered over 11,000.[17] Eighty Lockheed C-130 Hercules turboprops of the US Air Force, Douglas C-124 Globemasters of the US Military Air Transport Service (MATS), and ten DC-3s were involved in transporting these troops.[18] These aircraft also participated in Operation New Tape and Operation SAFARI: the largest United States Air Force (USAF) airlifts since the Berlin blockade of 1948–1949. Both the 322nd and 1602nd Air Divisions based at Evreux-Fauville and Chateauroux in France took part. They airlifted over 1,000 tons of food and over 2,500 refugees.[19] Soviet planes were also used in the transport of troops. Five Ilyushin-18 turboprops carried in food donated by the USSR and they transported Ghanaian troops from Accra to Leopoldville.[20]

Whereas the presence of UN peacekeepers brought the hope that the Congo might sail into calmer waters, barely two weeks had passed before yet another storm appeared on the horizon and threw Congolese politics into further disarray. Coming in the shape of Albert Kalonji, another of Lumumba's political rivals, his announcement on 8 August that the South Kasai was seceding came as a further blow to the prime minister. Again, Lumumba would make serious mistakes as he sought to uphold his economic strategy and force the diamond-mining region to abandon its plans.

The Secession of South Kasai

Situated to the east of the Congolese capital and bordering both Angola and Katanga, the South Kasai lay in the south-eastern corner of the Kasai region and was known for its large reserves of both gem quality and industrial diamonds. The secession of this 'diamond state' was driven by three interrelated factors: the conflict between the Luba and Lulua peoples; ideological opposition between the separatist Albert Kalonji and the unitary Lumumba; and the control over diamonds.[21]

Troops of the Swedish ONUC-contingent with two of their Terrängbil m/42D armoured trucks.

Provinces of the Congo 1960-1963. (Map by Tom Cooper)

ethnic groups. Seen as far more productive than the Lulua, the Baluba were separated from their hosts and were provided farming land in areas previously occupied solely by the Lulua.

The rise of Baluba elite over the previous decade or so made Belgian authorities fearful that its influence over political affairs and policies would become too influential. As a counterbalance to these elite, in 1952, the Belgians helped establish an ethnic association named the Lulua Frères. The increase in political awareness that took place during the next few years meant that the cleavage between Luba and Lulua grew. This took place in a context in which provincial authorities had suggested that around 100,000 Luba farmers in the flourishing centre of the Kasai be sent back to the impoverished south. Albert Kalonji led Luba opposition to this plan through organised demonstrations. Despite disputes inside the MNC in 1958 which had led to the creation of Kalonji's MNC-K, Lumumba, the leader of the MNC-Lumumba went to Kasai to demand his release. Increasing tensions between the Luba and Lulua would ultimately lead to armed conflict between the two groups and on 11 October 1959 estimates put the number of dead at between 3-7,000 as ethnic cleansing by the Lulua was carried out.[22] Conflict continued into 1960 and up to the general elections in May of that year and divisions were to worsen when Lumumba, as leader of the provincial government, decided to take sides by naming Barthélemy Mukenge, a Lulua, as president of the Kasai province. His doing so displeased Kalonji and the Baluba people he represented as they feared more persecution.[23]

To escape the Arab-Swahili slave raids that took place in the late 1800s, thousands of Baluba people fled south-eastern Kasai and settled in the Luluabourg (Kananga) and Luebo areas of the western Kasai. Welcomed at first by the Lulua, and integrating well into their communities, land and labour policies implemented by Belgian authorities in the 1920s began to create tensions between the two

A full 16 days before the independence of the Congo, Kalonji declared that the South Kasai would become a separate province and that it would secede from the Kasai as a whole. Accusing Lumumba of attempting to set up a 'communist dictatorship' in the Congo,[24] secession became 'official' and this new entity became the Mining

State of South Kasai, or the Autonomous State of South Kasai, with Bakwanga (Mbuji-Mayi) as its capital. Kalonji was named as its president and Joseph Ngalula its prime minister.[25]

Successive secessions were bound to anger Lumumba who saw unity between the Congo's peoples and those throughout Africa as the only means by which colonialism could be defeated.[26] As Kalonji attempted to gain support from Tshombe and the Belgians for his regime, over the coming days a series of discussions took place between Lumumba and UN Secretary-General Dag Hammarskjöld. Drawing on Resolution 143 and the mention that the UN would 'provide the Government (of the Republic of the Congo) with such military assistance as may be necessary', and that this assistance was to be provided 'in consultation' with the Congo government, Lumumba believed that the role of the United Nations was not to act as a neutral organisation but one which would put all its military resources at the government's disposal.[27] Hammarskjöld, on the other hand had a different interpretation of this mention. He believed that the role of the UN in the Congo was not to form an alliance of forces to be used against the secessionists but to ensure peace in the Congo and to preserve its integrity. In this respect the UN security forces could only use military force if they came under attack.[28]

In the face of Hammarskjöld's interpretation and needing to find a way to impose government authority the frustrated Lumumba decided to take matters into his own hands. His next decision would prove to be catastrophic in terms of his and the Congo's immediate future. In the middle of July, Lumumba turned towards the Soviet Union for assistance and, very shortly, weapons transported from Poland appeared in the Congo.[29] On 25 August, transported by Soviet planes, manned by Soviet technicians, backup crews and interpreters,[30] 200 men of the ANC left Ndjili Airport, Kinshasa for Luluabourg.[31] On 26 August, reportedly led by Czech and Guinean officers,[32] reinforced ANC forces now numbering around 1,000 wreaked a bloody reprisal on unarmed civilians: in Miabi 80 civilians were massacred;[33] hundreds of demonstrating Baluba were imprisoned and 70 of them were executed at Bena Makala. Killings also took place in Tshimbulu and Mwene Ditu, two villages around Bakwanga and in Benzola, around 1,200 civilians were massacred; 5,000 were killed at Kasengulu; and there were many other examples of the indiscriminate killing of unarmed individuals reported in the Congolese press.[34] Continuing conflict up to December 1960 led to a famine affecting around 300,000 refugees fleeing fighting and the UN estimated that up to 200 people died from hunger every day.[35]

Once Kalonji had resisted Lumumba's attempt to defeat the secession and had established himself through Luba support, he set about setting up the institutions which he believed would assure the future of his breakaway state. With state revenues put at some $30 million annually,[36] South Kasai became a functioning, though

Patrice Lumumba (centre, with glasses), with the General Secretary of the UN, Dag Hammarskjöld (light suit).

unrecognised state, and was equipped with a bicameral parliament, its own flag, and even its own stamps.[37] It had its own gendarmerie of around 3,000 members assisted by Europeans,[38] and these forces were used freely to maintain control and to further Kalonji's influence into neighbouring areas of the Kasai.[39] Increasingly militaristic in nature, the South Kasai imposed its authority by waging war against any ethnic group unwilling to accept Luba authority. In particular, military repression concerned the Kanyok.[40]

Considered by western powers as a bulwark to communist expansion in Central Africa, like Tshombe, Albert Kalonji received political and financial assistance from the moment of its creation. Forminière was one of South Kasai's largest financial sponsors,[41] and it received the support of South Africa, France and the Central African Federation (CAF).[42] Despite this support, the secession of South Kasai only lasted for around two years. Problems for Kalonji started when he declared himself the 'King' or Mulopwe of South Kasai.[43] These problems were further compounded when he was heavily criticised for taking personal advantage of a political situation.[44] A mixture of political pressure which saw Kalonji arrested in December 1961, UN military pressure and a military coup in September 1962 saw an end to the secession of South Kasai. The majority of its armed forces were integrated into the ANC.

Mobutu's Coup d'Etat and the Death of Lumumba

Back in Leopoldville in August 1960, Lumumba's political authority was further weakened when eight USAF crewmembers taking part in Operation New Tape were mistaken for Belgians, hauled from their aircraft at Stanleyville on 27 August and severely beaten.[45] This incident led US Ambassador Clare Timberlake to declare that the Congolese government had no control over the country and that it was attempting to regain this control with 'armed savage bandits'.[46] Dag Hammarskjöld would even go so far as to describe Lumumba's actions as 'genocide'.[47]

The ethnic cleansing that was also taking place in Northern Katanga against the Baluba and Lumumba's inability to maintain control eventually led to a constitutional crisis that would see Lumumba dismissed by Kasa-Vubu and replaced by fellow

ABAKO member Joseph Ileo.⁴⁸ Dismissing Kasa-Vubu in a show of his own constitutional powers, Lumumba accused the Congolese president of being 'a lackey of imperialism and Flemings';⁴⁹ accused the United Nations of working in conjunction with Kasa-Vubu to overthrow him; and accused UN official Andrew Cordier of playing a major role in the conspiracy.

Following a speech given on 7 September, Lumumba won an important victory when the Congolese parliament voted to annul Kasa-Vubu's decision.⁵⁰ Having gained parliamentary support Lumumba then turned his attention to the UN which he denounced by declaring that it was interfering in the internal affairs of the Congo and that any criticism directed against him by the UN was all part of a fascist campaign to get rid of him.⁵¹ Victories in the lower and upper houses of parliament also spurred Lumumba into demanding that UN forces be withdrawn immediately if it did not put an end to its 'occupation' of the airports and the national radio station.⁵²

Joseph Mobutu (second from right), was promoted from non-commissioned officer to colonel, and then Chief-of-Staff, ANC – all within just a few months in 1960. He eventually enacted the coup d'état that would make him president, in 1965.

Watching events unfold was Army Chief of Staff Joseph Mobutu. Sometime before 14 September 1960, the former Force Publique sergeant major stood in the doorway of Larry Devlin's office in Léopoldville declaring that he was 'anxious' to speak to the Chief of Station. Mobutu was concerned about what he termed as Lumumba and Kasa-Vubu's 'political games' and that they were not the way to create a 'strong, independent, democratic Congo'.⁵³ Concerned also about the presence of Soviet troops on Congolese soil and producing examples of alleged Soviet propaganda, Mobutu talked of an earlier conversation he had had with Lumumba during which he warned the Prime Minister to keep the Soviets away from the Congolese army. Claiming to have the support of his area commanders, Mobutu told Devlin of his intention to 'neutralize' Lumumba and Kasa-Vubu in an army coup d'état. The only condition was that the United States had to provide Mobutu with support.⁵⁴ The news that a plan was at hand to overthrow Lumumba was greeted as a blessing for an Eisenhower administration that had grown increasingly wary of the potential for communist-bloc intervention in the Congo. Communist ideology had held much attraction for African nationalists: from an economic point of view, the transformation

Mobutu reviewing a parade of ANC troops in Leopoldville.

of the Soviet Union had shown them what could be achieved in a relatively short space of time; and from a political point of view, its condemnation of Western imperialism in sub-Saharan Africa matched those elicited in the tenets of Pan-Africanism.

Pan-Africanism had come to be considered as a threat to US interests, both on international and on domestic levels. During a time when racial tensions and calls for civil rights for African-Americans in the US were on the increase, the Mau-Mau Rebellion in Kenya came to be considered by many in the United States as 'bloody retribution for the centuries of slaving and colonialism that Europeans had visited upon Africans'. However, it created the fear in Washington that the stark scenes of violence witnessed in Kenya would soon grip the United States'.⁵⁵

US concerns centred on its belief that Lumumba held communist sympathies. In this respect, it thought, Lumumba as Prime Minister

Lumumba is detained by the ANC before being taken to Katanga, January 1961.

Patrice Lumumba's brother, Louis, was also arrested by the ANC.

would not sufficiently represent US interests and goals in the sub-Sahara. This belief had led US authorities to put in place a political action programme designed to support pro-Western candidates in the legislative elections of May 1960 in order to 'marginalise Marxist groups' in the Congo.[56] Although there is no evidence to suggest that any political action had an effect on the results of these elections, in the two months following the independence of the Congo, it became increasingly clear to US national security policy-makers that Lumumba had used the constitution to set up a situation in which he held substantial political strength with support from the Soviet Union. Although Devlin did not believe that Lumumba himself was a communist, he was convinced that the Congo's Prime Minister was being manipulated by the Soviets and that eventually Lumumba would fall under their control.[57] Confirmation of this belief was given in a cable sent to CIA headquarters on 18 August 1960 when the US embassy and CIA officials stated that the Congo was 'experiencing [a] classic communist effort [to] takeover (sic) [the] government'[58] and that Lumumba was a 'stalking horse for what appeared to be a Soviet invasion.[59] Lumumba was also described as being 'crazy', having a 'particularly violent character',[60] and of being Africa's Castro.[61] Devlin advocated Lumumba's removal lest the Congo become another Cuba.[62]

Whether or not US perceptions of Lumumba's character were correct,[63] from mid-August 1960 the CIA started to draw up operational plans with the objective of removing Lumumba from a position of power and to replace him with a pro-Western group.[64] In late August, Devlin reported to Chief of the Africa Division Bronson Tweedy and informed him that anti-Lumumba leaders had approached President Kasa-Vubu with the plan. For the reason that nobody else in the Congo had Lumumba's political stature in his opinion, the president had refused to give his consent.[65]

On receiving a copy of Devlin's cable, the Director of Central Intelligence (DCI) Allen Dulles called a meeting of the Special Group, a subcommittee of the National Security Council responsible for the planning of covert operations. On 25 August, it was agreed that no measure should be ruled out when it came to the question of removing Lumumba. His fate seemed to be sealed when Allen Dulles himself became involved in the assassination plot and addressing a cable to Devlin, Dulles concluded that if Lumumba continued to hold high office the result would be chaos for the Congo and that this would pave the way for a communist takeover.

Lumumba's removal became a prime objective for Dulles and he was soon to authorise the expenditure of up to $100,000 to achieve it.[66] On 7 September 1960, the CIA was to make its first contact with Mobutu at the Presidential Palace. With political wrangling continuing over the next week or so, on 14 September Mobutu launched his coup d'état and announced that he was replacing the government with what was later to be known as the College of

Lumumba, Maurice Mpolo and Joseph Okito were severely beaten on the aircraft taking them to Katanga – directly in front of the UN peacekeepers and representatives of the international media.

The arrest and murder of Patrice Lumumba provoked a world-wide outrage. Those taking part in this demonstration in New York already knew about the involvement of their government in the Congo.

Commissioners. Moreover, in a move that was to please US officials, Mobutu also ordered the Soviet and Czechoslovakian Embassies to close, giving them 48 hours to leave the country.[67]

As a demonstration of what he called 'Christian clemency', on 24 September, Mobutu released Antoine Gizenga and Maurice Mpolo.[68] Both were close to Lumumba and following his arrest had attempted to organise a mutiny of the ANC in an attempt to bring down Mobutu. Mobutu also released Major Vital Jakasa, an officer of the ANC who had tried to assassinate him a few days earlier. Despite his arrest and his being placed in custody, the CIA still considered that Lumumba constituted a threat and it was concluded that the only solution to this was to remove Lumumba from the scene at the 'soonest' possible opportunity.[69] To do so, in mid-September 1960 the CIA asked one of its scientists, Joseph Scheider, to obtain 'toxic biological materials'[70] and on 19 September Devlin received a cable from headquarters informing him that another CIA employee codenamed 'Joe from Paris'[71] would arrive in Léopoldville a week later. Though Devlin claimed surprise at being told of the plot to kill Lumumba and stated that unseating him through parliamentary means was his preferred option, he was told that Eisenhower himself had ordered Lumumba's assassination.[72] Having earlier prepared hypodermic needles, rubber gloves, and gauze masks that were to be used when handling what was described as 'pretty dangerous material',[73] Gottleib handed over several poisons. One contained in a tube of toothpaste was intended to make it appear that Lumumba had died from polio but Devlin was told that he was free to use any method he considered effective. The only proviso, he was also told, was that the cause of Lumumba's death could not be traced back to the US government.[74] Lumumba was spared death through intoxication by Devlin's belief that the plot to kill Lumumba was 'both wrong, stupid, and a desperate plan that could easily go awry and devastate American influence in Africa'.[75] Ultimately, Lumumba was not killed by the CIA but by supporters of Moïse Tshombe on 17 January 1961.

On 27 November 1960, a banquet was organised at the presidential palace to celebrate Kasa-Vubu's return to power. On the other side of Kinshasa, Lumumba had managed to escape the gaze of the UN soldiers guarding his residence and was attempting to join supporters including Antoine Gizenga in Stanleyville in the Oriente province. Though over the next four days there was no sign of the former Prime Minister, there were reports that Lumumba had arrived in Kikwit in the Kwilu province and that he would attempt to reach north Kasai where members of his own tribe, the Batetela, would protect him. The prospect of Lumumba arriving in Stanleyville had emboldened his supporters in the city and on 28 November, they had beaten hundreds of Europeans still residing in the area. Around 1,000 of them were evacuated the following day.[76] On 2 December, the ANC announced that they had captured Lumumba in the Kasai and that he would be sent back to Leopoldville for trial. He arrived in the capital on later that day and had been visibly beaten. Held in the garrison cells at the ANC camp in Thysville until 13 January 1961, after another mutiny had enabled Lumumba to enjoy a few hours of freedom before being recaptured, the decision was made to send him to Bakwanga where the Baluba were eager to make him pay for the massacre carried out by ANC forces in August 1960. Accompanied by Maurice Mpolo and Joseph Okito, two men who had been arrested with Lumumba, the three were then taken to Lukala where they were picked up by a small plane operated by Belgian-owned Air Brousse. This aircraft took them to Moanda on the Atlantic coast of the DRC where then were then picked up by an Air Congo DC-4. Midway, the pilot was ordered not to take the prisoners to Bakwanga but to take them to Elisabethville instead. Revenge for Bakwanga came through the five hours of beatings the three men received during the flight from their Baluba guards. More beatings awaited them on their arrival in Elisabethville and a UN enquiry established that all three were shot shortly after their arrival on 17 January 1961. According to reports Katangan officials and Belgian mercenaries killed Lumumba and it has been said that Katangan Interior Minister Godefroid Munongo took part in the murders.[77]

4
Political Insurgency in Stanleyville, 1960-1961

Although from mid-September 1960 Lumumba was denied the possibility of exerting any direct influence over the political affairs of the Congo, his political allies and supporters known as 'Lumumbists' made determined efforts to ensure that he had some form of indirect representation. At the heart of this campaign was Antoine Gizenga. Described in some circles as 'very quiet', 'almost subdued', 'smart' and 'ruthless',[1] Gizenga was a strong advocate of using armed force to rid the Congo of its enemies. For example, as Belgian forces sought to quell the ANC mutiny in early July 1960, Deputy Prime Minister, Gizenga made an appeal to Nkrumah to send Ghanaian armed forces to the Congo in order to expel them.[2] Openly left-leaning and a founding member of the PSA, Gizenga never attempted to hide his sympathies for the Soviet Union and its ideology. His visits to Moscow and to the Prague Institute for African Affairs in Czechoslovakia for political training in the 1950s[3] convinced US officials that Gizenga should either be arrested or disposed of permanently.[4]

As Lumumba continued to be held under house arrest by UN guards throughout October 1960, Gizenga made his way to the MNC stronghold of Stanleyville from where he intended to mount political opposition to the Leopoldville regime. Joined by Lumumba's former secretary Bernard Salumu and Lumumba's brother Louis, this revolutionary triumvirate organised a mutiny of the ANC at the end of the month,[5] and in late November Gizenga received further backing for their breakaway regime when the recently deposed chief of the ANC, General Victor Lundula, promised his support.[6]

The intention and direction of Gizenga's regime were made very clear on 8 December 1960. As the UN's Sixth Security Council Meeting debated the circumstances surrounding Lumumba's arrest, on 8 December Salumu issued a declaration that all Belgians living in Stanleyville would be arrested and killed if Lumumba was not released within 48 hours.[7] Since the beginning of September, Europeans and UN peacekeepers had come under attack from 'Lumumbists'. While negotiations to guarantee fair treatment of the hostages continued in New York, Gizenga again illustrated his communist sympathies on 13 December when he made a declaration to the President of the Security Council – Soviet Valerian Zorin – that the 'lawful government' had been moved to Stanleyville, and that the Free Republic of the Congo had been created.[8] Other former members of Lumumba's government then attempted to join him: these included former Minister of Youth, Maurice Mpolo; Minister of Information, Anicet Kashamura; former Minister of the Interior, Christophe Gbenye, and Pierre Mulele who was to become the regime's Foreign Minister. Further political support came from the Belgian Communist Party (BCP) who, as early as November 1960, had reportedly been providing assistance to Gizenga.[9]

Though, militarily, Gizenga could count on a degree of support from Lundula, Gizenga lacked the equipment that would enable him to counter the ground attacks being made by Mobutu's ANC.

Intelligence reports about the Soviets channelling funding for Gizenga led to such incidents as when the ANC arrested a group of Sudanese UN peacekeepers in the port of Matadi, as documented by this photograph.

Although some reports state that on 15 December, an Ilyushin-14 cargo plane had transported weapons and other material into Stanleyville[10] it has been suggested that Khrushchev had become wary of supplying military aid to the Congo,[11] and that the United States had already taken measures to ensure that supply routes through Sudan had been blocked.[12] Attempts by other sympathisers to supply Gizenga's government with weapons and advisors were also thwarted: Nasser refused to allow a Czech delegation to cross Egyptian air space, and a second Soviet consignment of weapons that was due to be sent through Ghana never arrived.[13] There are, on the other hand, plenty of sources that confirm Khrushchev did supply financial aid. In the interest of paying his troops the same as those in Mobutu's forces Gizenga was provided with $500,000[14] and the CIA also claimed that another $500,000 payment was intercepted by agents in Sudan. This money was to end up in the general fund of the US Treasury.[15]

In regards of a seemingly never-ending succession of insurrections that have regularly punctuated the recent history of the DRC, the so-called Lumumbist rebellion was a relatively short-lived affair. Analysts of the events that unfolded from 26 December 1960 were, nevertheless, concerned that the establishment of Gizenga's rebel government was a symptom of the civil authority being exercised in a haphazard, arbitrary and sometimes violent fashion and that tribal warfare and blood feuds were likely to lead to more widespread disorders. There was no indication that the Congo was developing a leader who could unite the nation as a whole and develop a national consciousness, and this political instability was seen as the vector through which organised and disorganised violence and other excesses appeared to be the most likely prospect for some time to come. The presence of UN forces did provide a degree of public order and it would prevent outside powers from seeking to exploit what was evidently a power vacuum.[16] One particular problem which alarmed US Department of State analysts was that it was becoming increasingly sceptical about the capability of Mobutu's ANC to do anything to stop the spread of rebellion. Furthermore, the loyalty of ANC troops to any given side in a conflict was seen as 'tenuous and fluid'. They did not like to fight, they did not like to be on the losing side and they were willing to serve whichever side would pay them the most. These three factors undoubtedly convinced many ANC to swop allegiances as funds to pay recruits were provided to Gizenga and territorial advances began to be made.[17]

While the Balubakat Youth continued to commit atrocities across northern Katanga, Gizenga's first military objective was to advance to Bukavu situated on the banks of Lake Kivu and unite with Baluba forces loyal to Sendwe and Anicet Kashamura, the founder of the CEREA party and former Minister of Information in Lumumba's deposed government. Once this objective had been achieved, the plan was to meet up in Manano[18] with more Baluba loyal to Laurent-Désiré Kabila. During the last two weeks of December, Gizenga's army of around 5,000 troops[19] consolidated its hold over the Orientale Province and on Christmas Day 1960, a small number of them marched into Bukavu on the southern tip of Lake Kivu. Meeting no resistance from UN peacekeepers stationed in the area or from a garrison of ANC troops normally loyal to Mobutu, Gizenga's forces headed south to the important tin-mining town of Manono. During the capture of this objective on 7-8 January 1961, Katangese Gendarmes defending the town were mutilated before being killed,[20] and after Manono was declared the capital of a new province called North Katanga. Meanwhile, other units of Gizenga's army moved west into the Equateur Province.[21] With Mobutu's ANC seemingly presenting no effective counterforce, and with

Katangan Gendarmes seen during their counter-offensive against Gizenga's forces in February 1961.

reports that Egyptian military advisors had arrived in Stanleyville, there were fears that the Congo would become permanently divided and that the Congo would become the scene of protracted East-West conflict.[22] An example of how ineffective Mobutu's forces were came on 1 January 1961 when 60 ANC soldiers sent to liberate Bukavu discovered that a garrison supposedly loyal to Mobutu was, in fact, loyal to Gizenga. Instead of fighting, the 60 men decided to surrender and lay down their weapons.[23]

The Stanleyville rebellion was to reach its greatest geographical extent at the end of February 1961 when forces loyal to Gizenga seized Goma on the northern banks of Lake Kivu and Luluabourg in the Kasai.[24] By then, however, there were signs – again linked to the question of loyalty – that Gizenga's military fortunes might be changing: ANC troops briefly loyal to Gizenga once again switched sides due to their not being paid while others deserted en masse.[25] Confirmation that they had switched sides came shortly after when Moïse Tshombe's forces launched a counter-offensive on 11 February 1961, and when Katangese Gendarmes and 400-500 mercenaries launched a counter-offensive.[26] The first Balubakat-held town to fall was Mukalakulu to the west of the Upemba National Park, then came Manono on 30 March. Katangan forces led by Major J. Matthys inflicted countless casualties,[27] and the capture of Manono put an end to all Baluba resistance in Katanga. From the beginning of April 1961, thousands of them fled to Elisabethville to seek the protection of the UN[28] whose troops had been authorised to use force against warring factions through Security Council Resolution 161 of 21 February 1961.[29] Approved by Hammarskjöld on 26 April, the resolutions also gave UN peacekeepers the authority to arrest and repatriate all foreign personnel in the Congo.

As the influence of the UN over Congolese internal affairs gradually increased, so did the concerns of Kasa-Vubu, new Prime

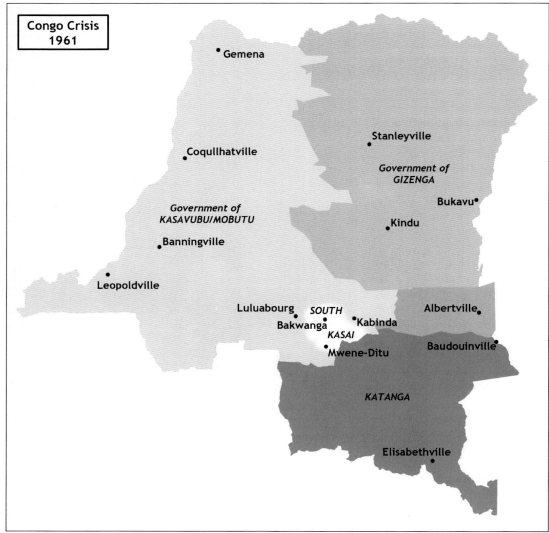

Divisions in the Congo in 1961. (Map by Tom Cooper)

Irish troops disgorging from the forward cargo doors of a giant C-124 Globemaster transport of the US Air Force.

Minister Joseph Ileo, Albert Kalonji and Moïse Tshombe. Instead of welcoming a larger UN military presence, they feared that the loss of Belgian military advisors and a disarming of their troops would open the way for Gizenga to impose his form of government on them, and that they would be tried for Lumumba's murder.[30] At a meeting between these leaders held in Elisabethville towards the end of February 1961, it was agreed that they should form a military pact aimed at stopping a 'communist tyranny and United Nations tutelage'.[31] To allay these fears, it was also agreed that they should meet in Tananarive in Madagascar on 5 March and that Gizenga should be invited.[32] Hosted by Malagasy President Philibert Tsiranana, Gizenga showed his disdain for the talks by denouncing them as a meeting of 'traitors and puppets'. He demanded that parliament should be reconvened and that the Stanleyville government be recognised as the only legitimate authority.[33] In response, Gizenga's opponents demanded the suspension of Resolution 161 and argued that the Congo no longer needed the UN to settle its affairs.[34]

Though Gizenga believed that he could continue Lumumba's legacy, it was clear that he could not command the same type of loyalty and respect as had the deceased former Prime Minister. This could be witnessed through Gizenga's failure to acquire the kind of popular support which would enable him to mount sustained military action against Leopoldville, and his failure to convince international supporters that he could assume the mantle of a revolutionary leader. Aid promised by Egypt, by the United Arab Republic and Czechoslovakia for Gizenga's regime failed to materialise despite Mulele's visits to

The Irish Army contingent initially arrived woefully ill-equipped: even their uniforms were too thick for the conditions found in the Congo, and their transport consisted of old and unprotected Willys Jeeps and Land Rovers. After one of their patrols was ambushed by Baluba tribesmen in Niemba, on 8 November 1960, leaving nine troops dead, the Irish Army rushed eight Ford armoured cars to reinforce its contingent.

Moscow and Prague in March 1961,[35] and even Lumumba's most influential international ally, Kwame Nkrumah, seemed to be turning his back on the Stanleyville regime. Though Nkrumah expressed his desire to see the Congo run by the Congolese during a meeting with US President Kennedy in Washington DC in early March 1961, he also expressed some contempt for Gizenga's 'abilities and suitability as a leader'.[36] Refusing to transfer to Stanleyville a consignment of Soviet weapons that had arrived in Accra in December 1960,[37] Nkrumah's about-face on the subject of support for Gizenga can be explained by his courting the United States, the United Kingdom and the World Bank in order to obtain funding for the Volta River Hydroelectric Project.[38]

Diplomatic efforts led by Hammarskjöld and various authorities in the Congo would finally lead to an end to the Stanleyville regime. On 12 May 1961, Kasa-Vubu announced that the Congolese parliament would be reconvened under UN guidance, and this was an initiative for which Gizenga gave his support. The UN then arranged for delegates from Leopoldville and Stanleyville to meet at the UNOC operations centre on 13 June, and here they agreed that Parliament would gather at the University of Lovanium from 16 July. Hopes

As the situation in the Congo worsened, the Irish quickly applied makeshift camouflage on their Ford armoured cars, usually by daubing them with mud.

Ghanaian peacekeepers on arrival in Leopoldville.

that the Congo would find political and social stability through a coalition of different parties were raised when Cyrille Adoula of the MNC-K was invited to form a government on 2 August. Including a number of Lumumba supporters in his cabinet with Balubakat leader Jason Sendwe and Antoine Gizenga both becoming deputy prime ministers, Adoula stated that his government would draw up a new constitution, ensure the observance of fundamental freedoms, and maintain law and order. He added that his government would strive to work hand-in-hand with the UN and adopted a resolution that as long as the Leopoldville government continued to receive votes of confidence from Parliament, no other government could claim to act as such. Adoula's government of national unity would be the legal successor to the first Central Government of the Republic of the Congo. Hammarskjöld expressed his satisfaction at the outcome of negotiations and the forming of a new government. He was invited to attend a meeting with the Congolese government on 10 September 1960, and three days later the Secretary-General arrived in Leopoldville. As well as discussing the framework within which support for Adoula could be provided, the most pressing issue was bringing secessionist Katanga back into the Congolese political and economic folds.[39]

5
Political and Military Insurgency in Katanga, 1960-1963

If India was once considered as the 'Jewel in the Crown' of the British Empire, Katanga was certainly Belgium's most valuable colonial asset in terms of what minerals could be extracted from its subsoil. This was confirmed just two years after its takeover of the province from Leopold II by UMHK's future administrator Professor Henri Buttgenbach. In a report presented to the Belgian Society of Engineers and Industrialists in 1908, Buttgenbach spoke of how, previously, he had predicted that Katanga would soon become one of the largest producers of minerals in the world. He also spoke of how some suggested that his predictions might have been rather hopeful and that Katanga's geographical position presented an insurmountable barrier to Belgium ever being able to fully take financial advantage. Ever confident in his research, Buttgenbach pointed out to sceptics that, yes, they were right to allude to the difficult terrain, and that the near absence of infrastructure would severely hinder attempts to transport riches from the interior. Indeed, he reminded them that on a previous visit to Katanga in 1902, it had taken him four months to reach his destination. However, he also reminded them of how, in 1850, California could only be reached after an eight-month sea voyage, how the path to the Klondike had been nicknamed 'The Road of Death', and how, only 20 years ago, it had taken three months of travel along a waterless and shadeless route to reach the Transvaal. Buttgenbach indicated that, contrary to other parts of the Congo, Katanga's climate was mild and that the average temperature was 21°, and that the vast plateaux covering Katanga resembled those found in the Ardennes region of Belgium. Frequently swept by trade winds, the malaria-carrying mosquitoes that blighted the rest of Africa could not settle. These conditions meant that the number of white settlers in Katanga had increased regularly since 1900 and, in that time, only two people had died. Neither of the deaths was linked to the climate, and nobody had left Katanga because of malarial fever. For Buttgenbach, there was no obstacle to the Katanga becoming a colony similar to Rhodesia, a colony in which 14,000 whites now resided.[1]

As we saw in a previous chapter, over the coming 50 years, the Belgian government made great use of the Congo's hydrographic network to facilitate transportation: the Congo River would be used to ferry red rubber and ivory out of the interior to ports situated on the Atlantic Ocean, and its tributaries which snaked throughout the Congo Basin and beyond would provide early options to traders wishing to transfer their wares to Europe.

Another mining engineer, Sir Robert Williams, was central to the development of other means of transport necessary for the transfer of Katanga's minerals to ocean destinations. An advisor to Cecil Rhodes, Williams starting planning the construction of the Benguela railway after the death of Rhodes in 1902. In conjunction with projects put in place by the BCK, a company created in 1906, by 1929, the Benguela railway would provide a link that stretched from the port of Lobito in Angola all the way to the copper mines of Kolwezi, and the rail networks of southern Africa.[2]

When Leopold II discovered that he needed an injection of capital to start mining operations he signed an agreement which conceded a third of Katanga's total surface of nearly half a million square kilometres to a private consortium called the Katanga Company. The CSK was then created to handle the province's administrative affairs and did so until 1933. In 1900, the CSK granted British company, Tanganyika Concessions, the right to carry out mineralogical research in the southern extremes of the province. The immediate discovery of deposits of tin and copper led to TCL forming a partnership with Société Générale and, together, they created the UMHK in 1906. Mining activities carried out by UMHK were undoubtedly the most important factor in determining the socio-economic landscape of the province supplemented by the Compagnie du Congo pour le Commerce et l'Industrie (CCCI), Forminière and Gécamines. From an economic point of view, extracting 80% of all minerals[3] UMHK's profits from the mining of minerals including cobalt and uranium grew to some 3.5 billion Belgian francs in 1959 and, as for the province's population, it had grown to 1.6 million. As of 30 June 1960, one-fifth of this population was European.[4]

As is the case with all Congolese provinces, Katanga was tribally diverse with the Lunda and the Luba forming the principle tribal complexes. Not limited to the boundaries of the eastern province, the Lunda Empire of Mwata Yamvo extended to the Kwango District in the Leopoldville Province, to Kasai and western Katanga, to the Lunda and Moxico Provinces of Angola and to the Balovale District in what was then Northern Rhodesia. A second Lunda empire, that of Mwata Kazembe was to be found in the south-eastern areas of Katanga contiguous to the Luapula River and lakes Mweru and Bangwelo. Other tribes found in these areas sometimes called the Congo Pedicle are the Bemba and the Lamba. The Luba Empire extended from Northern Rhodesia (Zambia) through central and northern Katanga into the Kasai.[5]

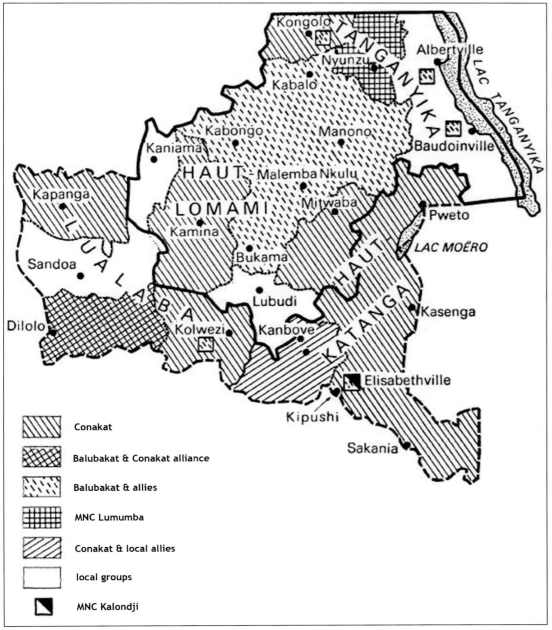

Tribal Divisions in Katanga. (via author)

Indigenous migration to Katanga was spurred by the socio-economic opportunities offered by economic development. By 1959, 36% of Katanga's population worked in the mining industry,[6] and the 200,000 residents of Elisabethville represented 52 African tribes almost entirely non-native to the city.[7] Half the city's residents were members of Northern Katanga's Luba tribe or from Luba areas in Kasai, and there were also significant communities of Chokwe, Bemba, Lamba, Lulua, and Songye. Similar tribal communities could be found in Jadotville, Kolwezi or in smaller Katangan towns such as Kisenge.[8] Where such tribal diversity existed, it is not surprising that when given the opportunity to do so voting was carried out along tribal lines: a familiar pattern across the Congo as a whole. The first test of how Katanga's inhabitants intended to vote came in 1957 during municipal elections which were held in December.

From 1891 to the 1920s, the Congo had been divided into small administrative units called *chefferies*, and later *secteurs*[9] controlled by village chiefs or chiefs of a given territory. Changes to this structure came firstly when Minister Louis Frank accorded limited powers to town councils; and, secondly, when the demographic shift to urban areas of the post-war period called for more town planning. The burgeoning political ambitions of a younger, more educated class of Congolese also influenced the decision to overhaul the system. Up to 1957, councils comprised members nominated by the Governor-General or the provincial governor, but after December of that year, members would be councillors elected from candidates representing social, economic or cultural groups.[10]

All Belgian or Congolese males over the age of 25 were given the right to vote in these elections, the first of which were held in Leopoldville, Elisabethville and Jadotville.[11] As mentioned above, voting respected tribal divisions rather than voting for a political programme, and though candidates often described themselves as supporters of particular ideologies, more often or not, they had no political programme.[12]

One Congolese who did have a manifesto was Jason Sendwe. A member of the Luba tribe from Katanga's Kabongo Territory, in 1957 Sendwe founded the Balubakat. As the name indicates, this was an association which represented the Luba, or Baluba, in Katanga. In 1961, the number of Luba residing in the province was between 280-300,000.[13] Noted by the Belgian authorities for their prolificity, and their rapid acceptance of European values such as gaining an education, in the 1940s and 1950s many Luba made their way to from Kasai to Katanga in search of employment. Through their propensity for work, and through their being more qualified than the Lunda, the Kasai Luba attained a higher social standing than the other groups and were often found working in offices or in banks.[14] The Luba in northern Katanga, on the other hand, were highly disadvantaged. Living in areas where they were less likely to have access to employment in the mines of southern Katanga, they found hope in Sendwe's Balubakat which was wholly committed to providing the Luba with more political power.

The success of Kasai Luba during the municipal elections (three out of four burgomasters) came as quite a shock for Moïse Tshombe. Tribally opposed to the Kasai Luba, and wanting to avoid any future political domination, Tshombe and fellow *évolués* Godefroid Munongo, Evariste Kimba, and Rodolphe Yav created the Conakat.[15] This was a confederation of tribal associations representing more than 600,000 members who believed that the wealth of Katanga

Moise Tshombe (centre), self-imposed leader of Katanga during the first half of the 1960s, with General Noronha (right), Commander-in-Chief of the UN peacekeepers in the Congo.

should be reserved for those native to the province.[16] Coming to represent what Kasa-Vubu's government would describe as a 'bastion of Belgian paternalism in the Congo',[17] Tshombe's family had benefitted greatly from the economic development carried out by Belgium in Katanga. Born in Musumba in southern Katanga in 1919, Tshombe was the son of the man who was reputed to be the Congo's first native millionaire. Having received his education at Methodist missions in Sandoa and Kanene, Tshombe was to qualify as an accountant before completing a rise to the top of Katanganese when he married into the family of Mwata Yamvo, the chief of the Lunda tribe. After relocating to Elisabethville in 1946, in the early 1950s Tshombe continued to pursue his business interests. Though, at this time, he was financially secure, his inability to contract loans from banks purely because he was a native Congolese encouraged Tshombe to take his first steps into politics. With help provided by his father-in-law, from 1951-1953 Tshombe served as a member of the Provincial Council of Katanga before serving on the permanent delegation of the Government Council in the province.[18]

Though its mandate was to promote the interests of different tribes in Katanga – including the Balubakat – political movements representing European settlers quickly identified Conakat as the party that would help them achieve the goal of setting up a regime functioning along the lines of that in South Africa, or forming a union with Rhodesia.[19] The most influential of these groups was the Katanga Union (Union Katanganaise, UK) presided by Achille Gavage. Supporting Conakat's political doctrine that the Congo should be comprised of a federation, and that Katanga should maintain close links with Belgium, it affiliated itself with Tshombe's party in 1959 through the hope that it could gain the trust of native Katangans, and through the hope that it could influence the Round Table discussions due to be held in Brussels in December of that year.[20] Eventually taking place in January and February 1960, 45 Congolese delegates left the meetings having negotiated complete independence which would take place in June 1960. Even before negotiations had commenced, there were signs of discord among the leaders of the associations that allied with Conakat. In particular, the reference to 'authentic Katangans' in its manifesto raised suspicions amongst the Luba and the Chokwe that they risked becoming the poor men in any government that Tshombe might form.

As a demonstration of their opposition, towards the end of November 1959 both the Luba and the Chokwe seceded from the Conakat. Forming a new Luba alliance composed of the Balubakat, the Fédération des Associations de Ressortissants du Kasaï au Katanga (FEDEKA) led by Albert Kalonji,[21] and the Association of Tshokwe of Katanga and Rhodesia (ATCAR)[22] in December. Although, it also wanted to see the setting up of centrally-led federation of six Congolese provinces with as much autonomy as possible, it opposed the idea of separatism. According to Jason Sendwe, this would lead to the suicide of the Congolese nation.[23] Sendwe's beliefs explain why in December 1959, the Cartel approached leaders of the Abako, the MNC, and the PSA to form a united front against Tshombe in Brussels.[24]

The strength of the tribal and political divisions which existed between the peoples of Katanga, once again, became clear when the Cartel and Conakat came head-to-head in provincial elections held in December 1959. Marked by a very high rate of participation (81.7% of eligible voters), over 82% of Katangans voted in accordance to their tribal affiliation or for independent candidates. The Conakat obtained 10.82% of the votes, while the Cartel obtained just 3.89%. In terms of the results, Conakat stated that it had won 427 seats out of 484. Its calculations were based on adding the number of seats it had obtained (84) to those of the Lulua-frères (7), those obtained by independent candidates standing for 'customary' traditions (191), and those standing for matters of local or independent interests (144). The Balubakat, which obtained only around 30 seats made strong appeals against these calculations. It argued that it was at a disadvantage due to tribal voting, and that it had only been able to stand in larger urban areas. This notion was supported by 21 of its 30 seats being obtained in Elisabethville.[25]

Having emerged triumphant from these elections, Tshombe returned to Katanga on 10 January 1960 where he was greeted by cheering crowds. Celebrations were soured, however, when Jason Sendwe was appointed Burgomaster of Elisabethville on 12 January: violence broke out between opposing supporters and a curfew had to be imposed by local police forces. More violence of a similar nature occurred in Jadotville on 31 January where four people were left dead.[26]

Despite what was a highly-divisive position, Tshombe remained firm in his belief that Katanga should be independent in some shape or form and that, in order to avoid the Congo becoming a dictatorship, Belgium should keep control of the Congo's finances and its foreign policy. He also suggested that the resources of each individual province should be their own.[27] Repeating his ideals in a second policy statement issued before parliamentary elections held in May 1960, Tshombe stated that:

> The Katanga is opting for an autonomous and federal state in which the reins of political authority would be in the hands of the

Katangans themselves and in the hands of all men of good will who have shown by their acts that they are collaborating sincerely with them for progress and the rapid emancipation of the Katanga, in accordance with conditions which will be determined by the future government of the Katangan State.[28]

Though it is not clear who exactly Tshombe meant by 'men of good will' and those who were his 'collaborators', suspicions that the Conakat was controlled by UMHK[29] were seemingly confirmed when the mining giant provided Tshombe with a loan of some 1,250 million Belgian francs.[30] This loan was joined by offers of financial and diplomatic assistance from Sir Roy Welensky who, as Prime Minister of the Federation of Rhodesia and Nyasaland, was to suggest that Katanga become a member of the Central African Federation. Others who were to lend support were Northern Rhodesia's United National Independence Party (UNIP)[31] Captain Charles Waterhouse, the Chairman of Tanganyika Concessions, Lord Robins of the British South Africa Party, and Lords Selborne and Clitheroe, both investors in companies associated with UMHK.[32]

With this high-level back up from what was termed by the Economist as the 'Katanga Lobby',[33] Conakat approached elections in May 1960 with a great deal of optimism. While this optimism was proved to be justified when Conakat won 45 of the 60 seats on offer, criticism of the way in which Belgian authorities had administered procedures came, unsurprisingly, from the Cartel. The problem this time, it explained, was not with Tshombe, but with the Belgians themselves. Results, it claimed, had been falsified; and political preference had been given to Tshombe through the banning of Sendwe from attending meetings at Baluba tribal centres, notably in Kamina. Though Belgian authorities admitted that there had been irregularities, it failed to put in place an enquiry due to the date of independence approaching rapidly. Receiving this news the Cartel decided not to take their seats at the Provincial Assembly, but its absence from the law-making process meant that the Conakat could not make or pass laws. This issue was overcome when the Belgian parliament authorised an amendment to the law-making process:[34] it effectively excluded the Luba from having any form of representation in the Katangan parliament and left the Conakat in a position of total political dominance over the province. Now holding the reins of power, Tshombe made his first attempt to secede just a few days before the independence of the Congo. On 25 June, Tshombe appointed Belgian businessman Frans Scheerlink as Ambassador of the State of Katanga. Handing him the mission of informing King Baudouin and Prime Minister Eyskens that Belgian authority was to be transferred over to Katanga, the ambassador was, henceforth, to represent Katangese interests at the United Nations in New York. Despite Belgium not being in the strongest position to mount a challenge to Tshombe and Munongo's decree, it was able to exert enough pressure to overturn the appointment by 27 June.[35] The second, and most successful, attempt at secession took place only a matter of days later.

To understand events which unfolded in the days leading up to the secession of Katanga, it is important that we briefly examine the psychological climate created by forthcoming independence. As political independence was being granted against the will of the coloniser, it should firstly be pointed out that there was a great deal of mistrust between Belgian and Congolese authorities. Though the Congolese had been given independence, they were not sure of the extent to which they were still bound to the Belgian administration assisting in the transition of power and, as for the Belgians, they were not sure that they had sufficient means to influence when it came to the question of protecting their interests.[36] Despite substantial goodwill on both sides to see the transition of power take place as smoothly as possible, Lumumba's speech at the Palais de la Nation and General Janssen's declaration to the Force Publique were to serve as tinder for the breakdown in relations between former coloniser and former colonised.

As we saw earlier, the mutiny by the Force Publique would lead to a small-scale exodus of Europeans (and Congolese) from the Congo as they sought refuge in neighbouring countries. In Katanga, the situation was no different. Hundreds of white settlers fled to the Congo's border with Northern Rhodesia where they were welcomed and given shelter by Welensky's authorities, but some who were unfortunate enough not to have made their escape were either butchered or shot. In Elisabethville alone, five Europeans including the Italian vice-consul were to suffer this fate. Diplomatic breakdown became complete when Minister of Defence Arthur Gilson ordered Belgian paratroops to restore order in the Katangan capital. Though Lumumba gave his blessing for an agreement that would see Belgian troops stationed for two months in Luluabourg to protect Belgian citizens, Tshombe saw the mutiny as no more than 'tactics calculated to create disorder and terror' instigated repeatedly in many countries now under communist dictatorships. Making accusations that the May elections had been fraudulent, and that they had left many provinces governed by a single party, Tshombe also accused Lumumba of constituting an 'extremist majority' in the central government and interfering in the internal affairs of the Katanga Province.[37] The latter referred to Lumumba's appointment of Jason Sendwe as High Commissioner for Katanga. Tshombe also noted in his declaration that the 'sole desire of the present Central Government [was] the disintegration of all the military and administrative machinery' and the 'establishment of a regime of terror that [would] bring about the flight of our Belgian collaborators'. Furthermore, the regime wished by this method 'to replace their trained men as fast as possible with staff personnel which the Government [had] already recruited from countries under communist domination'. For Tshombe, 'the Katanga could not lend itself to actions of this kind.' In his view, 'the government of the Katanga [had] been elected by a provincial assembly which itself was elected on the basis of a programme of peace and order', and 'these circumstances', Tshombe believed, 'would lead to the Katanga facing a threat to its welfare and to its being governed by the arbitrary and communist-inclined will of the Central Government'. For this reason, the government of Katanga was proclaiming its own independence: independence, in Tshombe's words that was 'complete'.[38] To protect Katanga from the 'communist-inclined will of the Central Government', Tshombe proclaimed the independence of Katanga on 11 July and called on Belgium to provide technical, financial and military help. Failing this Katanga would make an appeal to the free world to recognise its right to self-determination.[39] President Kasa-Vubu and Lumumba attempted to resolve the crisis by setting up a meeting with Tshombe and Munongo in Elisabethville on 12 July. However, as the plane was about to start its descent the pilot discovered that the order had been given to turn off the runway's landing lights. This gave him no choice but to return to Luluabourg and it seemed, at this point, that the reconciliation of the Congo would be impossible.

Katanga's Military Forces

Political separation from the chaos reigning over large parts of the Congo, the task that now befell Katangan authorities was upholding state integrity and warding off attempts to bring the newly-created

Colonel Jean-Marie Crevecoeur and Major Guy Weber.

Katanganese Gendarmes.

The Katanganese Gendarmes were officered by mercenaries recruited by Moïse Tshombe.

state back into the fold. The most immediate threat was posed by Jason Sendwe's Balubakat which objected to the unilateral declaration and which staged an armed revolt in the mining centre of Manano in northern Katanga. Soon, Tshombe would have to face Lumumba's ANC, the Stanleyville ANC, and UN peacekeepers authorised to use armed force.

Despite Belgium not recognising Katanga as an independent state until 14 July and its breaking of diplomatic relations with Lumumba's government, reports arriving in Brussels that Soviet military equipment had been delivered to Stanleyville spurred Belgian Prime Minister Pierre Wigny into authorising his deputy chief of staff, Count Harold d'Aspremont Lynden, to head the Belgian Technical Delegation (MISTEBEL) to Katanga.[40] D'Aspremont Lyndon's first steps on his arrival on 22 July consisted of putting in place the services which would provide public information and State security.[41] From an administrative point of view, the task of setting up structures such as a national bank and a communications network was facilitated by a good number of Belgian civil servants deciding to remain in Katanga to assist Tshombe. The same was true when it came to the question of defending Katangan integrity: Guy Weber – the commander of Belgian forces sent to evacuate its citizens a few days previously – became Tshombe's military advisor, and 250 members of his force were appointed to form the officer corps of a newly-created unit called the Katangese Gendarmerie. Commanded by former Force Publique officer, Lieutenant-Colonel Jean-Marie Crèvecoeur, the ranks of the gendarmerie were filled by tribesmen from the Bayeke and Bazela tribes.[42] Based at Camp Simonet in Elisabethville, or in

Kaminaville, Kabongo, Manono and Kabalo,[43] these ranks were to increase in number after a purge of ANC soldiers based in Katanga saw the recruitment of 3-400 soldiers willing to pledge allegiance to Tshombe.[44] In addition to this readily available stock of military manpower, Katanga could rely on a number of internal and external sources to build up its armoury of weapons and other forms of hardware. President Antonio de Oliveira Salazar of Portugal is said to have supplied weapons at an early stage,[45] and Belgian equipment, including a number of aircraft, was already to be found at Kamina Air Base.

The presence of these aircraft served as an enormous boost to Katangan ground forces. Fighting off continued attacks from the Balubakat Youth throughout August, the gendarmes gained air support for their operations through the creation of the Force Aérienne Katangaise (FAK), or Avikat. Created on 23 August 1960 using aircraft previously used by the air wing of the Force Publique (Avimil or Avi/FP) and headed by the latter's commanding officer, a Belgian named Victor Volant, the composition of its personnel bore witness to the ease with which mercenary pilots from a variety of backgrounds could be recruited. Operating mainly out of Luano Airfield in Elisabethville, but also out of Kolwezi, Jadotville, Kisenge, Dilolo and Kipushi, Volant could count on the experience of fellow Belgians Joseph Delin and José Magain, as well as Poles Jan Zumbach,[46] Stefan Wojcik and Witold Lanowski, Sandor Gyurkits from Hungary; a South African named Jerry Puren,[47] Jean-Marie Ngosa, a native Katangan, and a Trinidadian named Hubert Fauntleroy Julian. Though there is much intrigue surrounding the recruitment of these pilots, the latter's case is particularly interesting. Nicknamed the 'Black Eagle of Harlem', Hubert Julian acquired this sobriquet after he had flown over a meeting of the Negro Improvement Association headed by Marcus Garvey. The 'Black Eagle' had flown aircraft for Haile Selassie, had taken part in operations against Jacobo Arbenz in 1954, and had flown for Batista's forces against Fidel Castro.[48]

Supplemented by a team of aircraft technicians and mechanics recruited through adverts placed in French newspapers such as the *Dépêche de Toulouse,*[49] it is equally evident that aircraft were easy to come by and, seemingly, that no questions of a moral nature were raised by their suppliers. In addition to the British-produced De Havilland DH.114 Herons and DH.104 Doves, the US-made Sikorsky S-55 helicopters, and the French-made Aérospatiale SE.313A Alouette II helicopters already at Katanga's disposal,[50] Tshombe's agents were then able to acquire Vampire bombers, Douglas DC-3s, various Piper aircraft and North American T-6 Harvard's.[51] Through Cassart, the Avikat also gained German-produced Dornier Do.28s.[52] With the exception of the Vampires, all of these reached the breakaway province. However, Katanga's most significant acquisition in regards of its overall airpower was that of nine French-manufactured Fouga CM.170 Magister armed trainers.

A patrol of Katangese Gendarmes gets underway in two M38 jeeps.

Chris Souris was a member of the Katanganese Gendarmerie.

Sold by France to the Belgian Air Force, in December 1960 three of these were then loaded on to a Boeing YC-97 Stratofreighter registered N9540C owned by a CIA front company named the Seven Seas Charter Company,[53] or Airline,[54] before being flown to Luxembourg (where the front company was based), Malta and finally Elisabethville.[55] This assistance given by the CIA to Tshombe underlines how much Eisenhower's approach to the crisis and America's position in sub-Saharan Africa differed from Kennedy's. As for France, with South Africa preparing to become a republic, supplying weapons was a means of increasing its influence in anglophone and lusophone Africa hence the appearance of a number

Table 2: The Force Aérienne Katangaise, 1960-1963[56]		
Type of Aircraft	Number of Aircraft	Serials
De Havilland Heron	1	KAT-01
Douglas DC-3	3	KAT-02, -03, -04
Piper PA-22	1	7-4
De Havilland Dove	9	14, 15, 16, 17, 18, 19, 20, 21, 22
North American T-6C	11	KA-22, -25, -26, -27, -28, -29, -30, -31, -32, -33, -34
Sikorsky S-55	1	KAT-42
Alouette II	1	KAT-52, -53
Piper 95 Super Cub	1	KAT-61
Piper Tripacer	1	72
Fouga CM.170 Magister	3	91, 92, 93
Piper PA-24 Comanche	1	KA-119
Dornier Do.28	5	KA-3016, 3017, 3018, 3019, 3020

Child soldiers were a common feature of conflict in the Congo.

A third Fouga CM.170 Magister arrives in Katanga bearing its new serial number and roundel. Many aircraft of the Katanganese Air Force were acquired by former Belgian Colonel, Jean Cassart.

of French-produced weapons and aircraft in conflicts fought by South Africa and Rhodesia.

The increasing nature of the threat to Belgian lives and to Katanga was to encourage large numbers of former servicemen from Belgium, other parts of Europe, and South Africa to travel to Katanga to offer their support. In July 1960, members of two groups opposed to King Baudouin, the Comité d'action et de défense des Belges d'Afrique (CABDA) and the Corps Franc Roi Baudouin (CFRB) set up the so-called Tshombe Brigade.[57] Jean Cassart, formerly of the Special Operations Executive (SOE) was able to recruit around 30 parachutists: these former legionnaires or veterans of the Korean War were offered a renewable six-month contract with a salary of up to 15-25,000 Belgian francs per month.[58] Another recruiter was Charles Lambert, the owner of the Café Edelweiss, who was able to recruit a further 20 men for the Tshombe Brigade.[59] Tshombe also sent recruiting missions to Belgium on 18 September and was able to supplement his forces with a 180 mercenaries, officers and NCOs.[60]

As far as the actual fighting was concerned, as with similar asymmetric wars in Indochina or Algeria, the tactics of the Balubakat Youth relied on terrorising local populations in order to gain their loyalty, then making attacks on isolated, small units of opposing forces. This was the case in Manano on 5 September when Balubakat forces led by Lievin Nyembo overran a column of Gendarmes in Manano.[61] Next, with the objective of dismantling Katanga's administrative infrastructure, the same forces attacked and killed officials in the Bukama territory of the Lualaba department on 13 September. They continued by killing dozens of people in villages such as Mukula Kula.[62] Further atrocities were reported in early October when an unknown number of civilians including Europeans were massacred by the Baluba in the Kabalo region;[63] and when 15 tribal notables and teachers accused of belonging to Conakat are beaten and executed at Manano in mid-November. The dead include hereditary chiefs Vincent Yangala, Norbert Kisimba and Bernard Kaboko.[64]

Retribution for these attacks came swiftly and they demonstrated that Tshombe's forces could meet terror with terror. At Luena, on 15-16 September, Katangese gendarmes opened fire on crowds gathered waiting for trains leading to a number of casualties, and in the coming hours they spread out across the surrounding areas. The gendarmes arrested and killed 68 villagers who turned out to be Baluba warriors.[65] Twenty more Baluba are killed at Mitwaba on 1 October.[66] Throughout August and September 1960, it has been estimated the Baluba suffered up to 7,000 casualties.[67]

Katanganese Gendarmes come into contact with forces of the Balubakat in northern Katanga.

Villages suspected of harbouring Balubakat sympathisers were shown no mercy by Tshombe's forces.

In addition to casualties inflicted by the gendarmes, mercenary groups organised into small units called Groupes Mobiles also roamed around the Katangan bush in Minerva or Willys jeeps armed with .30 calibre machine guns and trucks armed with recoilless guns, while the troops carried Belgian FAL 7.62mm rifles or Vigneron 9mm submachine guns. The job of these Mobile Groups was to patrol areas where local intelligence had indicated the presence of Baluba. A village suspected of harbouring enemy soldiers and feeding them as they moved southwards towards Elisabethville would be burned to the ground, its livestock killed or eaten, and meagre belongings destroyed. If any Baluba were detected by mercenaries in rebel-held areas around Kabalo, Manono, Malemba-Nkula, Luena or Bukama, they were dealt with in the same manner they had used on local inhabitants or Europeans.[68] For this reason, mercenaries operating around the Kongolo region became known as Les Affreux.[69]

As we saw earlier, in January 1961, the Baluba Youth were joined in their fight against Tshombe by ANC soldiers loyal to Patrice Lumumba. With four distinct armies now present in the Congo, fighting spread eastwards from the Kasai to the north of the Upemba National Park to areas situated along Lake Tanganyika and northwards towards Burundi and Rwanda.[70] While counter-attacks organised by Tshombe's forces included a raid by the Katangese air force on Manano on 30 January,[71] larger counter-offensives codenamed Banquise, Mambo and X-Ray took place under the command of Lieutenant-Colonel Frédéric Vandewalle from 10 February-6 May

A typical column of a Groupe Mobile gets underway during a raid in late 1960.

The Compagnie Internationale or White Legion, Katanga 1961. (Nigel Osborn)

1961.[72] As a former officer of the Force Publique, Vandewalle had been given overall command of Mistebel in November 1960. His appointment came after officials in Brussels began to have doubts about the effectiveness of the management of Weber, Crèvecoeur and defence advisor André Grandjean, and internal disputes between the three were worsened by Tshombe's belief that his indigenous troops were ill-disciplined, were becoming increasingly involved in tribal disputes, and were mistrustful towards white officers.[73]

Whether or not this mistrust was generated by the legacy left behind by Force Publique attitudes towards the native soldier is a matter of debate. What we do know is that in early January 1961, Katangan authorities sought to replace Jean-Marie Crèvecoeur with a high-ranking French officer and to recruit a hundred or so French or German junior officers.[74] The man seen as being the most suitable to take overall command of Katanga's armed forces was Colonel Roger Trinquier. A veteran of the Second World War, the First Indochinese War, and the Algerian War, Trinquier was also a leading figure in the May 1958 coup that had brought De Gaulle back to power.[75] Renowned as a specialist in the theories of counterinsurgency, and author of a military manual used by armies around the world,[76] on 5 January 1961 Trinquier received a letter from Katangan official George Thyssens whom Trinquier was to meet in Nice a week later. At a meeting with French Minister for the Armed Forces, Pierre Messmer, in Paris on 15 January, it was explained to Trinquier how much France could benefit from having an officer of his calibre in this part of Central Africa. Despite opposition from the French Ministry for Foreign Affairs, Trinquier arrived in Elisabethville some ten days later and accepted Tshombe's offer to take command of his forces. In order to evaluate Katanga's military needs, one of Trinquier's first tasks was to tour the zones where rebel activity had been at its strongest. Somewhat surprisingly given the number of attacks carried out by rebels in recent months, Trinquier's conclusion was that the war in Katanga had not truly started. This was because the Baluba had not yet been able to mount organised attacks and, because of this, Katanga's forces using traditional military methods and strategies had been able to fight them off. However, this situation would change as the rebels turned towards the use of methods favoured by revolutionary armies. These were methods that the rebels knew perfectly well but that regular forces had yet to acquire. Revolutionary warfare, according to Trinquier, did not consist of capturing military equipment or towns. Instead, its principal objective, as mentioned above, was to gain control over local populations using tactics such as building peaceful relations with local communities, infiltrating local political organisations, and gaining the type of influence that could be used to spread its ideology in larger towns. Once trust had been established, terror and brutality were used to create collective fear and submission. Trinquier had witnessed these methods during his service in Algeria. While the Front de Libération Nationale (FLN) had not seemed to pose a threat to French forces until July 1956, the explosions which took place in Algiers that month made the French realise that the FLN had gradually been building up its forces in the Algerian capital over the past 18 months and that they now faced 6,000 rebels intent on seizing power. Taking back control required six months of fighting by the 10th Parachute Division of which Trinquier was the deputy commander. Trinquier warned Tshombe that unless he equipped Katanga with the means to counter revolutionary warfare, within 18 months to two years bombs would be exploding in Elisabethville. Trinquier's plan consisted of putting together, over five years, a modern army adapted to conditions in the Congo, and adapted to modern warfare.⁷⁷ A mixture of animosity from Weber and Belgian opposition to French involvement in Katanga put an end to Trinquier's five-year plan. In spite of his return to France in March, Tshombe's wish to recruit a private army came to fruition through the creation of the Compagnie Internationale.

After replying to adverts placed in the South African or Southern Rhodesian press, potential recruits, such as former British serviceman Nigel Osborn, would be invited to an interview at recruiting centres in Johannesburg or in Salisbury (Harare). Informed that they would be required to take on policing duties, around 30 Europeans, South Africans and Rhodesians were selected. Offered six-month contracts with a salary of just over £100 per month by recruiters Charles Huyghe and/or Roderick Russell-Cargill, the Compagnie Internationale, or 'White Legion', as it was sometimes known, was transported to Elisabethville on regular flights operated by Belgian airline Sabena. Kitted out into uniforms once worn by Belgian forces in Katanga, the headgear of the Compagnie Internationale resembled the bush hat worn by Australian forces. Though it was based in Shinkolobwe, an important mining town some 200kms north-east of the capital, the Compagnie Internationale's policing duties also extended to Baluba as far as Mitwaba, Kongolo or Kabalo.⁷⁸ Generally speaking, the involvement of the company in the fighting was limited to localised skirmishes or arresting suspected Balubakat, but on one occasion it distinguished itself in Manano working in conjunction with Katangese gendarmes.⁷⁹ Undoubtedly one of the most short-lived units to have served in Katanga, the Compagnie Internationale's time in the Congo came when its members were arrested and repatriated by Ethiopian troops of the UN's peacekeeping force. Many of those arriving in Katanga in March and April 1961 had been in the province for barely a month. A second attempt at recruiting an English-speaking and independent army took place at around the same time, and it was directed, again, by Huyghe and Cargill using the same advertising methods, offering the same contracts and similar rates of pay. Led by Irishman and former British army officer, Mike Hoare, 4 Commando was a 121-man unit bankrolled by UMHK. As was the case with groups of French-speaking mercenaries operating concurrently in Katanga – groups commanded by Jean Schramme or Robert Denard – 4 Commando would be forced out of the Congo in August and September 1961. Indeed, following the death of UN

UN peacekeepers arrest men of the Compagnie Internationale.

Offices of Radio Katanga after an attack by UN peacekeepers.

General-Secretary Dag Hammarskjöld in circumstances which are still to be fully explained, the UN appointed Burmese diplomat U Thant. Adopting a far more aggressive stance towards foreign combatants in the Congo, Thant authorised operations Rumpunch and Morthor. Finally putting down Katangan secession through Operation Grand Slam at the end of 1962, Tshombe handed back formal control of the province to Cyrille Adoula on 5 February 1963. Under increasing pressure from his political opponents, Tshombe found himself forced into exile in June 1963. However, this political insurrectionist would return to his homeland when other political insurrectionists once more posed a greater threat to the integrity of the Congo than ever seen before. This was the Kwilu rebellion.

6

The Chinese Method in Africa: the Kwilu Rebellion

The reintegration of economic powerhouse Katanga into the Congo offered the hope that the country might be able to move towards financial independence and prosperity. Being none too aware that more effort was necessary if the Congo was to avert further instances of anti-government protest, Prime Minister Adoula made attempts to bolster the efficiency of the ANC through the so-called 'Greene Plan' of July 1962[1] and, in August of the same year, brought in a law which would provide three new Congolese provinces. Conscious of the fact that rural areas were a potential source of political and economic discontent, the objective of this law was to partly decentralise governmental powers and to provide the new provinces with a greater amount of political autonomy. The three new provinces were the Kwango, Mai-Ndombe, and Kwilu provinces, the latter being the main focus of this chapter.

Kwilu Province

Consisting of high plateaux, deep, valleys, savannas, forests and palm groves, the borders of the Kwilu province remained roughly the same as what was known previously as the Kwilu District created in June 1960.[2] Divided into five territories (Kikwit, Idiofa, Gungu, Masi-Manimba, and Banningville), these borders were the River Kasai to the north, the River Kwango to the east, and the River Loange to the west. In May 1963, these five territories became prefectures, and a sixth – the Kamtsha-Loange – was added in June 1963. This was to satisfy the demands of the Ngoli people whose chiefs agreed to the creation of the Kwilu province only on the condition that this political subdivision would be respected.[3]

The Kwilu's population of 1.25 million in 1960 was sparsely spread over the 77,300kms of the province.[4] Even though, with 16 and sometimes 17 inhabitants per square kilometre, it was one of the more densely populated of all the Congo's provinces.[5] Residing, for example, in cylindrical-shaped huts topped with banana leaves, the population of the province was ethnically varied. This was particularly so in the north of the Kikwit territory where villages of the Nsongo, Yansi, Mbala and Hungana tribes were found either side by side. Other tribes found in the Kwilu were the Mbunda, the Dinga, the Shilele and the Pende. The latter was the most represented of the different ethnic groups and numbered 550,000 in 1960.[6]

Despite this mosaic of difference ethnical groups found in the Congo the tribes of the Kwilu had two things in common: most inhabitants spoke languages derived from Kikongo and there was widespread belief that all the Kwilu's peoples originally came from the Kwango. As these ethnological aspects provided a platform for unity, unlike other Congolese provinces, e.g. Katanga, the Kwilu saw relatively little hostility between its different tribes. This being said, the Pende tribe had a time-old tradition of challenging external attempts to subjugate its people and impose systems foreign to their customs. Illustrations of this resistance can be found with the Pende revolt and the fact that many of the Congo's most radical leaders belonged to this tribe.[7] These include Antoine Gizenga, the leader of the Stanleyville government and Pierre Mulele, the leader of the Kwilu rebellion.

Bearing in mind this history of protest, it should come as no surprise that the rural rebellion which began in earnest in January 1964 received such support from the Kwilu's population. It had seen

Pierre Mulele.

relative deprivation after the value of its crops dropped dramatically in the 1930s; earnings of harvesters had fallen by 50-60%; and, to cap this, colonial authorities were either oblivious or insensitive to the condition of the Kwilu's masses. Later, instead of the prosperity promised by independence from Belgium, these masses found that they were, once more, excluded and that little had changed as far as income and opportunity were concerned. Leopoldville, it appeared, governed by what has been referred to as a bourgeoisie monopolist;[8] and the state budget was being used not to improve areas such as social services, but was spent on building prisons, strengthening the armed forces and supporting the privileges of those elected to parliament.[9] In view of this situation, the question should not be centred on why the Kwilu Rebellion came about, but rather why a large-scale rural uprising had not eventuated long before. When Pierre Mulele promised his partisans that any government under his leadership would provide the Kwilu's residents with beautiful houses, free furniture and free petrol for their free cars, it is understandable that they were quick in rallying to his cause.[10] Another reason for Mulele's success is that he was able to exploit a context dominated by a system of tribal customs and beliefs in which the rhythm of daily life on a local level was determined by tribal chieftains. Though these leaders often held sway over the lives of hundreds, and sometimes, thousands of people, power was dispersed among many. The absence of centralised authority to organise and manage collective revolt explains why the Pende revolt was so short-lived. It also explains why political parties with centralised power such as the PSA were able to gain dominance over traditional power structures.[11] As we shall see, however, Mulele was able to exploit traditional beliefs, customs and structures to advance his own political ideology: Maoism. Let us now take a closer look at

Nearly all the parties involved in the Congo Crisis – including the Congolese armed forces, UN contingents (like that of the Irish Army) and the various mercenary units – made extensive use of such all-terrain utility vehicles as US-made Willys Jeeps (left) and British-made Land Rovers (right). The majority of these were left in dark green overall, and relatively few wore any kind of distinct markings other than their 'registrations'. Many were armed – usually by a single Browning .30 cal or 7.62mm machine gun, installed in front of the co-driver. The Land Rover shown to the right is a Series III and was operated by the Belgian Paras. (Artworks by David Bocquelet)

The Daimler Ferret armoured car was developed in the late 1940s as a light reconnaissance car for the British Army, and first entered service in 1952. Over 4,400 were manufactured in 16 variants by 1962, and 30 were acquired by the Congo. Additional Ferrets were then brought to the country by the Malaysian Special Force – the ONUC-contingent from that country. Drawn from C Squadron, 2nd Reconnaissance Regiment, the Ferrets in question were all left in dark green overall, as on delivery: some received the UN-crest in white on their turret sides, while a few wore 'personal' names, like 'Lily' in this case. This artwork shows the vehicle with its turret traversed 90 degrees left (i.e. showing the front side of the turret). (Artwork by David Bocquelet)

The Fabrique Nationale AS.24, was a foldable motorised tricycle, 460 of which were manufactured during the 1960s for use by the Belgian parachute troops. It was 85cm high, powered by an 15hp engine, had an empty weight of 170kg and could carry up to four passengers (including driver), or 350kg of equipment, at a maximum speed of 97km/h. Belgian paras deployed them during Operation Dragon Rouge in November 1964. The artwork here shows an AS.24 together with its cargo trailer. (Artwork by David Bocquelet)

While none of the ONUC-contingents is known to have deployed its own M3 White Scout Cars to the Congo, some of these were requisitioned from the ANC – which had received them from the Belgians – and then pressed into service by both the Katangan Gendarmes and the UN peacekeepers. This example was operated by the Swedes and received some camouflage colour sprayed on the sides, plus UN markings. There was no camouflage on the top of the engine cover: instead, it was marked with 'UN' in black. All Swedish-operated M3 White Scout Cars received personal names ending with 'Belle': this one was Olga Belle. (Artwork by David Bocquelet)

The 'off-road vehicle model 42' (Terrängbil m/42D) was designed by AB Landsverk on the chassis of a standard Volvo truck, and included an armoured superstructure for the crew of two and seven full-equipped infantrymen. Around 150 were manufactured in total, several of which were deployed with the Swedish ONUC-contingent in the Congo in 1961-1964, where they became known as 'white elephants' because of their overall white colour. Each vehicle was armed with one or two kspm/36 machine guns and had its front wheels partially protected and rear wheels almost completely covered by additional armour plates. (Artwork by David Bocquelet)

The Katangese Gendarmes operated at least two US-made M8 Greyhound armoured cars, taken over from the ANC. This example is known to have retained the original 37mm gun, but also received a high, cylinder-shaped extension to the turret for two machine guns, of which the 12.7mm Browning M1919 faced in the opposite direction to the main gun. Originally painted in green overall, this vehicle eventually received a camouflage pattern consisting of sand and dark brown, and a small Katangan flag (shown inset, upper left corner) high on the front of the left side of the turret. By the time it was photographed at Elisabethville in 1961, it had a second machine gun, of 7.62mm calibre, and an even more elaborate set of markings on the glacis (shown insert, left), including its 'registration', a white cross, and the number '9' on a yellow circle. (Artwork by David Bocquelet)

RIPE FOR REBELLION: POLITICAL AND MILITARY INSURGENCY IN THE CONGO, 1946-1964

This illustration shows a solider of the Armée Nationale Congolaise (ANC), as seen in action during one of the street battles of the early 1960s. He wears a plastic helmet-liner for the US-made M1 – which served more as a symbol of status than for protection – and the olive-green Force Publique M1955 tenue de combat uniform with a collarless jacket. The Belgian webbing was copied from the British 1937 Pattern, although only the canvas belt and a pouch magazine appear here. The rubber-soled boots and anklets also followed the British standard. While most of the Congolese combatants were armed with Belgian weapons, such as Vigneron machine guns, M1952 bolt-action Mausers and FN/FAL assault rifles, many also carried old British-made Lee Enfield rifles. (Artwork by Anderson Subtil)

The Swedish ONUC contingent was one of the first to enter Congo. The status of its troops was clearly identified by the blue helmets of the US M1 pattern, and the blue arm patch with white hemisphere and laurel leaves (right shoulder); with national insignia worn on the left shoulder. His combat uniform included a green drill shirt and trousers made of lightweight and fairly loose-fitting material to suit the local climatic conditions. The green webbing included two pouches for 36-round magazines for the 9mm Carl Gustav m/45 sub machine gun. His only other weapon was an old-fashioned Swedish M1915 bayonet. (Artwork by Anderson Subtil)

Major Mike 'Mad' Hoare commanded 5 Commando. This illustration shows him wearing a Belgian Army service shirt and British combat trousers. His belt was of British 1944 pattern, to which he added a Belgian Army holster for a Browning Hi-Power 9mm Parabellum pistol. Typically, the mercenaries in the Congo wore the rank insignia of the Belgian Army: in this case a single yellow bar and star of a Major. This was completed with a dagger symbol for the Commandos, all affixed on a green fabric slide. His headgear consisted of a commando green beret with ANC golden officer badge between the two bars. (Artwork by Anderson Subtil)

iii

This Simba rebel of the Armée Populaire de Libération (APL), in Stanleyville of 1964, is shown wearing a khaki shirt from the ANC and blue trousers made of reinforced fabric, probably from the stocks of a mining company. He has added whitened webbing and anklets form the Belgian Proveté Militaire (Military Police). Notable are the red fez from the Force Publique, duly decorated with an animal skin. His attire was completed through the addition of vegetation to the shoulders and classic Adidas sport-shoes. His weapon was a Belgian-made M1924/30 Mauser carbine. (Artwork by Anderson Subtil)

This illustration shows one of about 140 native officers of the Katangese armed forces in 1961. He is shown wearing a Belgian-made Denison-style camouflage smock and greyish trousers with two thigh pockets. The black combat boots, web anklets and belt were all British style, as was his field cap, which bore the enamelled brass badge of the Gendarmerie Katangaise. A metal grenade on a white disk on the red shoulder strap slides and a brass Katanga Cross identify him as a Sous-lieutenant of the Proveté Militaire Katangaise. The weapon shown here was the original version of the classic 7.62mm FN/FAL assault rifle, although most of the Katangese infantrymen were armed with older firearms, like the British Lee Enfield and Belgian versions of the Mauser carbine. (Artwork by Anderson Subtil)

This Belgian Paracommando of the 1er Bataillon Para, Régiment Para-Commando is shown wearing the Belgian maroon beret in British style, with a cap badge that alluded to the origins of the Belgian paratroopers who operated with the British Army during the Second World War. The Belgian combat smock design closely follwed the British Denison smock, and featured a subtle green, brown and olive camouflage. Following the same influence, his webbing was also based on the British 1937 Pattern and carried a holster for the classic Browning Hi-Power 9mm automatic pistol. (Artwork by Anderson Subtil)

RIPE FOR REBELLION: POLITICAL AND MILITARY INSURGENCY IN THE CONGO, 1946-1964

Like other aircraft of this type, and all the C-124s, this C-130A Hercules (full serial 55-006) of the 322nd Air Division (Military Air Transport Service, USAF) in mid-1960s was left in aluminium overall, but had large parts of the rear fuselage and the fin painted in dayglo orange. Due to heavy wear and the local climate, both the aluminium overall and the dayglo orange tended to appear rather dark. Large service titles and other insignia were all applied in black. The C-130s involved in Operation Dragon Rouge generally looked similar but without any dayglo orange surfaces: instead, they wore the large insignia of the 322nd Air Division, USAF, low on the undercarriage housing and often on their underwing drop tanks, and that of the Military Air Transport Service low on their fins. (Artwork by Tom Cooper)

The Swedish ONUC contingent initially deployed three Saab J.29B Tunnan fighters to the Congo, including aircraft marked as D (construction number 39374), E (29393), and F (29398). All three were initially left in their original, 'aluminium overall' livery, while wearing black markings, but had their national markings replaced by those of the UN. Their principal armament consisted of four 20mm internally installed Hispano Mk V automatic guns, but this could be enhanced through the addition of four launch rails for 75mm unguided rockets under each wing. (Artwork by Tom Cooper)

Due to the threat of Katangan air strikes, all of the J.29s deployed at the Kamina AB received camouflage patterns – which differed from aircraft to aircraft. This S29C (construction number 29944) was one of two examples of this reconnaissance variant flown by the Swedish ONUC contingent. Over-sprayed in green, green-blue, and tan on upper surfaces and sides, it had its undersides left in original aluminium overall, and received an 'identification strip' around the intake: this was actually an area of the original colour left unpainted. (Artwork by Tom Cooper)

v

The Indian Air Force contributed six Canberra B.(I).Mk58 to the UN's peacekeeping contingent. As usual for the time, all were left in highly-polished aluminium overall livery and, in addition to the standard set of national markings (including roundels applied in six positions), received big black titles 'ONU' on the rear fuselage. Notable is the gun-pod containing four 20mm Hispano Mk V cannons, installed in the gun bay. Their deployment was crucial for the destruction of the Avikat. IF908 survived two subsequent wars with Pakistan and remained in service with the IAF until 2004. (Artwork by Tom Cooper)

Between September 1961 and October 1962, the Imperial Ethiopian Air Force deployed four North American F-86F Sabre fighter-bombers with the UN peacekeepers in the Congo in support of some 3,000 Imperial Bodyguard personnel that served there. Drawn from the 1st Fighter-Interceptor Squadron, these initially operated out of Leopoldville, before moving to Kamina AB, from where they flew combat sorties in cooperation with the Swedish and Indians. Ethiopian Sabres were left in their aluminium overall colour and wore UN markings, including a small blue crest of the UN, on the fin: national markings were eventually removed. (Artwork by Tom Cooper)

Out of nine DH.104 Doves operated by the Avikat, details are known about at least five. Four of these wore the livery and markings similar to the example depicted here: white on upper surfaces of the fuselage and the fin, and either bare metal (covered by clear lacquer) or aluminium on sides and undersurfaces, engine nacelles, wing and horizontal stabilisers. The flag of Katanga served as a fin-flash, and the roundel was worn in six positions. The full serial – KAT-22 – was applied on the rear fuselage only: 22 was repeated under the left wing, inboard of the roundel. (Artwork by Tom Cooper)

RIPE FOR REBELLION: POLITICAL AND MILITARY INSURGENCY IN THE CONGO, 1946-1964

The T-6C KA-25 was the only Texan of the Avikat for which the original US serial number is definitely confirmed: 41-33752 (construction-number was 88-13598). This was the only example to become involved in an air combat – with a J29B of the Swedish UN contingent, on 29 December 1962, while flown by the Polish mercenary Stefan Wócjik. Photographs of this aircraft show it wearing two different camouflage patterns, but always carrying the nickname 'Penny' in white. This was the first of the two camouflage patterns, consisting of dark brown and dark green on upper surfaces and sides, and azur blue (FS 32250) on undersurfaces. The 'serial' was applied in white, by brush, and without the use of any kind of aids. (Artwork by Tom Cooper)

Amongst the Belgian aircraft taken over by the Avikat were two Sud-Est SE.3130 Alouette II helicopters (renamed Aérospatiale SA.313A Alouette II in 1967). Both were painted in dark green overall, and are known to have received full Avikat insignia, including white serials KAT-52 and KAT-53, and roundels on their sides. They primarily served for liaison purposes. (Artwork by Luca Canossa)

The last of three CM.170 Magisters of the Avikat that caused the UN so much trouble in September 1961 wore the serial 93. This reconstruction shows it as seen at Kolwezi airport in November 1961: it retained its aluminium overall livery, with dayglo-orange on the nose, wing-tip fuel tanks, intake-lips and a strip around the rear fuselage. The aircraft was at the time armed with a pair of 7.62mm machine guns in the nose: it received at least one underwing hardpoint under each wing, used for carriage of light bombs or – as shown here – a six-round pod for 68mm unguided rockets. This Magister was eventually evacuated to Angola in 1963. (Artwork by Tom Cooper)

Pierre Mulele (centre) with supporters in the Kwilu, sometime in 1963 or 1964. (Courtesy Aclhetron.com)

what made Mulele become such a powerful figure and how he was able to use his communist credentials to such great effect.

Who was Pierre Mulele?

Born in 1929 in the small village of Isulu-Matende in the Gungu territory Pierre Mulele's father, Benoît, was one of the first 'intellectuals' in the regions surrounding Idiofa just to the west of Kikwit. A nursing assistant, and husband to Agnès Mulele, Benoît was well-liked by the patients he helped to treat and passed on his desire to aid the poorest to his son Pierre. Instilling values he believed would make Pierre a good pupil at the local Catholic mission school, the Sacred Heart, Benoît began to teach his son the alphabet from a very young age. The Sacred Heart was just one of the Catholic schools that dotted the Congo's landscape and it provided the most immediate link between the country's children and the Belgian authorities. Providing schooling in French, the objective of the schools was to make a contribution to Belgium's mission of 'civilising' the Congo's population through literacy and discipline. While the Jesuit priests at Mulele's schools in Kikwit, Kinzambi or Leverville were devoted to their role and dedicated their time to the children's welfare, Mulele saw their intentions as nothing more than paternalist and made frequent challenges to their authority. In his eyes, there was little difference between the holier-than-thou discourse of the priests and those of the colonial authorities: the Congolese were being educated purely so that they could provide a workforce for the palm plantations, the railroads or the mines, and so the priests could not hope to spread the word of equality when they, themselves, were part of a system that promoted inequality. According to Mulele, when a system such of contradictions existed, and when the Congolese were forced to work for little pay through the persuasion of a whip, how could there not be an insurrection of the masses?[12]

On leaving technical school in Leverville in 1949, Mulele made his way west to the Yaeseke School of Agriculture situated in the Bumba Territory of the Equateur Province. In Yaeseke, Mulele was again to show his rebellious nature by boycotting lessons. Asked to explain his behaviour by the headmaster and told that he was jeopardising his future, Mulele said that he wanted to play no further part in a system which he saw as benefitting only the Belgian authorities. It is, therefore, quite surprising that in 1951 Mulele took the decision to join the Force Publique, the militia which the Congolese considered as the main tool of colonial repression. Arriving at Coquilhatville military camp sometime in 1951, Mulele's superiors soon took notice of his relative intelligence in relation to many of the recruits that formed the lower ranks. As a consequence, it was not long before Mulele was promoted to the rank of corporal and found himself working as deputy-secretary to the commanding officer: the first time a Congolese recruit had been entrusted with such a responsibility. It was an appointment proved to be a godsend for the future leader of the Kwilu rebellion as, igniting his interest in military history, Mulele took every opportunity to delve into the archives at the camp and to study reports on the quelling of different rebellions by the colonial armies. In particular, Mulele analysed how these forces had put down a revolt which had taken place at the Luluabourg camp in Elisabethville on 20 February 1944. This was the first organised effort by the Congolese to gain political control and represents an important episode in the development of Congolese nationalism.[13] Mulele concluded that the only reason the Force Publique existed was to crush any move towards independence. His interest in military history began to take a turning point at this stage, and self-education became a means by which Mulele could plan any future uprising. He studied maps, the localisation of different units of the Force Publique and the tactics it had used to maintain peace. He even drew up a plan which involved taking over the camp at Coquilhatville.[14]

When Mulele left the Force Publique in 1952 and settled back into civilian life, his attention turned to politics. By the end of that year Mulele had moved to Leopoldville and it was here with the help of former classmates such as Théodore Bengila and Fernand Nima that Mulele set up the Union des anciens élèves de la mission Leverville (UNAMIL), one of the first organisations of *évolués* in the Kwango-Kwilu region. Shortly after arriving in the capital in 1953, Mulele managed to join the civil service where he worked in the government's public works office, and in the same year he started to take an active interest in the Lumumba-led APIC. One of the aims of this movement was to obtain wage equality between black and white workers.[15] Inspired by Egyptian president Nasser's denunciation of British ambitions during the Suez Crisis of 1956 and by the FLN's revolutionary war in Algeria, Mulele was also enthused by Kwame Nkrumah's message in the quarterly cultural, political and literary magazine *Présence Africaine*, that nationalist Pan-Africanism and the desire for African emancipation should be spread to all the corners of the continent.[16]

Though Mulele had yet to become completely radicalised at this point and had not made calls for Congolese independence, an important step that set him on the path towards demanding that

Belgium leave the Congo took place in 1958 when, with several hundred other Congolese *évolués*, he was invited to attend the Brussels World's Fair. Also known as Expo '58, the Fair is probably best known for its purpose-built centre-piece called the Atonium. Organised to showcase technical and cultural visions of the future, Belgian representatives had, instead, decided to present its 'achievements' of the past and dedicated its pavilion to showing the world how Belgium had 'civilised' the Congo. Problems with Belgium's exhibits presented in an area supposedly representing a typical Congolese village arose almost immediately. At the entrance to the village, the Ministry of Colonies had placed a bust of King Leopold II, a scene which raised many eyebrows due to the atrocities his regime had committed; and to add insult to injury native art prepared by the Congolese had been rejected and replaced by exhibits made by Europeans. Worse was to come, however, when a certain number of *évolués* were required to dress in traditional Congolese attire.[17] This led to accusations that Belgium's ethnological exhibition was no more than a human zoo, and these accusations were supported by reports of spectators throwing money or bananas over the bamboo enclosure which ringed the Congolese pavilion. These racial insults added to cramped accommodation and restrictions imposed on the Congolese delegation forced the *évolués* to leave and return to the Congo.[18]

Fidel Castro was sympathetic to the cause of the CNL.

Though this spectacle caused uproar in international circles, Mulele took advantage of the situation to gather Marxist literature banned in the Congo to hone his political thought. Reading works such as Joseph Stalin's *The Foundation of Leninism*,[19] or the *Selected Works of Mao Tse-Tung*,[20] in 1958, Mulele also increased his knowledge of revolutionary doctrine when he met Vasilis Bouras of the Greek Communist Party. He would learn how the USSR overcame Nazi occupation, and how in the Soviet Union the interest of the collective came before the interests of the individual and that the workers controlled the means of production. Mulele was reminded of how Lever controlled the palm oil industry in the Congo and how Union Minière controlled the mining industry.[21] Impressed by the contents of dialogue, as Minister of Education in Lumumba's first government, Mulele would appoint Bouras as an advisor.[22]

As Mulele veered towards adopting a more radical political philosophy throughout 1958, the next important stage in his career took place in February 1959 following the creation of the PSA. Co-founded by Antoine Gizenga of a radical group called Action Socialiste and Sylvain Kama in Leopoldville, by May 1959 it had extended its activities to Kikwit in the Kwilu and had added labour union activist Cléophas Kamitatu to its numbers. Following this extension, Gizenga became the party committee's first president whereas Mulele was elected its Secretary-General and Kamitatu the president of the PSA's provincial branch.

Though the PSA drew most of its political representation from the Kwango and Kwilu provinces and focused much of its political activity on these two areas, the PSA was by no means a regional party. It saw itself as distinct from the existing political organisations such as the ABAKO or the MNC – which the PSA considered as too Conservative – and held ambitions of representing national interests. Perhaps the most over-riding distinction it made from Lumumba's MNC was that its leaders did not hail from the Leopoldville province. Instead, they came from the Equateur, Orientale (Lumumba) and the Kasai (Kalonji).[23] The main aim of the PSA as stated in their programme was the emancipation of Africans in all domains – the inclusion of this term demonstrating the racial, and not purely national, nature of the movement – and secondly, independence should be obtained in stages.[24] On a national level, its programme was populist in nature promising to end unemployment; build more schools and provide free education in rural areas; increase salaries; provide better housing in rural areas; and provide free medical care to all non-salaried citizens. Though these measures would not be considered as particularly radical in some modern democracies, the policies of non-alignment with European powers as well as the implementation of a socialist programme based on peasant collectives or traditional communal farms[25] put the PSA firmly in line with Stalinist and Maoist political doctrine.

Possessing a highly organised structure, and divided into three principal branches: the National Congress, the National Political Bureau, and the National Central Committee, the PSA benefitted from a leadership representing a wide range of political and labour organisations. Considered as a political bulwark against the tribalistic ABAKO, the PSA even gained the moral support from the traditional chiefs, or lembas, of ethnic groups in a minority in the Leopoldville Province. This was due to the diversity of the tribal affiliations within the party: Gizenga was a member of the Pende tribe, Mulele was an Mbunda, and Kamitatu was a Bangongo. In addition, the Bambunda, the Bambala, and the Mukongo were all represented in the committee of party officials based in Kikwit.[26] The multi-faceted nature of the PSA meant that its popularity grew rapidly and in the first two weeks of its creation it had collected 67,500 francs in dues from a range of people living in towns and villages, or from those living on plantations.[27] The PSA's popularity can also be put down to its manifesto for the elections of May 1960 in which it promised work for all, an increase in salaries, free schooling, free medical care for the non-salaried, and improved housing.

Despite being able to count on this diversity in the elections of May 1960, it soon became clear that an ideological schism existed within the PSA: Gizenga and Mulele favoured hard-line socialism while Kamitatu preferred a more moderate form of social democracy.[28] Though political differences threatened the future existence of the

PSA at this point, the composition of Lumumba's first government acted as a pacifier: Gizenga became Deputy Prime Minister, Mulele was nominated Minister for Education, and Kamitatu's committee was appointed to lead the provincial government. The next phase in the evolution of the PSA came in December 1960 when Gizenga established a breakaway government in Stanleyville and appointed Mulele as his Foreign Minister. As we saw earlier, the so-called Lovanium Conclave and Antoine Gizenga's decision to join Cyrille Adoula's reconciliation government in August 1961 brought hostilities between pro- and anti-government factions to an end. It was a fragile peace, however, and intra-party tensions increased when Gizenga was arrested and imprisoned in January 1962, and when a restructuring of the Congo's administrative landscape in September of that year saw the creation of the Kwilu Province. This led to the political moderate Norbert Leta, a Pende, being appointed as president of the province's first government, and led to Mulele hardening his political position.

The Causes of the Kwilu Rebellion

A reform of the Kwilu's administrative environment carried out by Leta and his provincial government was seen as a model for future economic development. However, there were soon signs that these policies did not meet with the approval of the rural population that found it having to pay more taxes or having to work for next to nothing on plantations. Regional authorities, it seemed, were insensitive to their plight and favoured the economic development of more urbanised areas such as Kikwit and Idiofa. Finally, it appeared to the rural masses that the prosperity promised by independence had passed them by.[29] This was true in many respects. Only around 150,000 Congolese are said to have benefitted materially from independence.[30]

For the majority of the Congo's population that worked long hours in low-paid jobs, life continued to resemble the same struggle it has always been. Inflation was on the rise with hundreds of millions of dollars being pumped into the economy; teachers and other low-ranking civil employees found their salaries frozen or not paid at all, and many low-paid officials and ordinary citizens turned to corruption to make ends meet.[31] Many even turned to diamond smuggling as a means of meeting their basic needs.[32] This bleak economic context was worsened by the arrival of rural populations into metropolitan areas such as Leopoldville and only served to add pressure to an already high level of unemployment. At the end of 1961, it was estimated that 51% of the male labour force in the capital was without work.[33] This is a staggering figure considering that within a year of independence, the population of Leopoldville had almost doubled from 378,158 to 733,170.[34]

When it came to the salaries of the army and the police, Adoula's government had made a particular effort to make sure that security forces remained loyal. Promising to increase army pay by 347% and police pay by 240% in comparison with pre-independence rates,[35] authorities undoubtedly sought to avoid the kind of mutiny which had taken place in July 1960, or the change of allegiance which saw hundreds of ANC soldiers switch sides and support Gizenga's Stanleyville government. However, as Claude Welch observes in his study on the origins of rebellion, 'a salary promised is not necessarily a salary delivered'.[36] In protest against arrears, 200 police forced their way into the town hall in Leopoldville on 3 May 1963. Then, taking 30 people hostage, the police made their way back to their camp at Lufungula. The protest only came to an end when gendarmes and paratroopers stormed the camp and forced the surrender of the mutineers. They were subsequently arrested and either imprisoned or repatriated as was the case with those originating from the Kwilu. Many were to join Mulele's forces some months later.[37]

Whereas disgruntlement over issues linked to pay was demonstrated through armed protest in Leopoldville, protest in the Kwilu in the spring and early summer of 1963 was more political in nature. Convinced that the political direction of the current government was being guided by the so-called Binza Group,[38] and was therefore favourable to the west, Gizenga's partisans (also referred to as the *jeunesse*) initiated small-scale protests against virtually anything they perceived as a symbol of the United States. These protests included assaulting a missionary who had given out sachets of powdered milk manufactured in the US and displaying anti-American propaganda in towns and villages. Slogans appearing on posters would tell of how the Congo had been sold to the Americans, how the Congo was now under US control, and how Adoula and his ministers were on the pay role of the CIA. Meanwhile, the poor were growing poorer. What Gizengists were proposing was a rejection of US money and the creation of a new political order that would benefit all Congolese, and not just a privileged few. Only Gizenga's PSA was capable of ringing in these changes.[39]

Though written protest can prove to be highly effective in certain societies, the low level of literacy of the Kwilu's population and its lack of political awareness meant that political change that would favour the poorest could only be brought about by gaining a majority in the provincial government or, in Mulele's case, by mounting a popular rebellion. In many respects, it would seem that the second of these options had been on the minds of Gizenga's supporters for some months before Mulele returned to the Congo in July 1963. Their refusal to attend the PSA congress held in June 1963 led to the pro-Adoula Théophile Kamitatu being re-elected as president of the provincial government; Kamitatu was then able to constitute a government whereby the majority Pende, Mbunda and Dinga were under-represented; and it enabled Kamitatu to distance pro-Gizenga supporters such as Sylvain Kama from positions in which they might be able to mount a political challenge. The distancing of potential threats to Kamitatu's authority extended to traditional centres of power and it was reported that tribal chieftains in Idiofa had been arrested and placed in detention.[40] Kamitatu also ordered the military to harass card-carrying Gizengists by regularly demanding identity papers. Failing this they were arrested and placed in detention.[41]

The Overall Objectives of the Rebellion

The strained political atmosphere that existed in the Kwilu in the summer of 1963, and the belief that there would be no change in the fortunes of the majority of its inhabitants, were godsends for an ardent revolutionary like Pierre Mulele. Ending a political exile which started in April 1962, and returning incognito to the Congo from the People's Republic of China (PRC), Mulele saw the situation as the perfect opportunity to implement what is sometimes referred to as the 'Chinese Method in the Heart of Africa'.[42] Adapted from Maoist military and political strategies he had acquired during training in Peking,[43] the fundamentals of Mulele's method contained the trusted communist strategies of convincing the rural population that only a revolution and the replacement of the current regime by a popular socialist government could bring the change they desired. Describing Adoula, his ministers, and supporters of the government as 'corrupt, treacherous brothers who were reactionaries of the bourgeoisie',[44] Mulele believed that the Congolese government was at the mercy of an international capitalist hegemony, and that its objective of 'deliberately raping' the Congo of its sovereignty and independence had to be stopped immediately.[45]

Though he had arrived in the Congo on 3 July 1963, it was not until the 1/2 August that he made his way to Nkata in the Kwilu. Accompanied by former schoolmates and fellow revolutionaries Théophile Bengila, Leonard Mitudidi, Thomas Mukwidi and Félix Mukulubundu, the first part of the plan consisted in dividing the Kwilu into smaller geographical units. Then establishing an operational base, the next step was to recruit and train partisans in order to carry out small-scale attacks on isolated pockets of enemy forces.[46] Using captured weapons, and recruiting more partisans, the rebel army would then attempt to seize control of small and medium-sized cities until the final objective of overthrowing the government had been achieved.[47]

Recruitment and Training of Mulelists

At the first meeting of Mulele's revolutionary executive held on 5 August 1963,[48] it was decided that training camps would be set up in Mbunda territories between Lukamba, Yassa-Lokwa and Imbongo.[49] The next step was to recruit partisans for the rebellion, and this was carried out in Mbunda, Pende and Dinga areas and by the end of August Mulele's forces, including 150 women had swelled to 580.[50] Among those first recruited were Bengila's brother Valère Etinka and Mulele's future wife, Léonie Abo.[51]

While it should be expected that the poorest inhabitants of the Kwilu would form the majority of recruits – especially after the ANC's violent repression of rebel activities in September[52] – the social backgrounds of those who chose to join Mulele was actually quite diverse. The same is true when it comes to the question of age: despite being referred to as the *jeunesse*, or youth, many were by no means young. Indeed, in Mulele's movement, the term *jeunesse* had a different meaning, and it was applied to those who were seen as being young and progressive in mind rather than being young in body.[53] It might also be expected that recruits to Mulele's army would derive from either his or Antoine Gizenga's tribes, the Mbunda and the Pende respectively. While this was also true, and while the Pende associated Mulele's rebellion with the Pende Revolt of 1931, there were a number of people from other tribes who answered the call. For one reason or another, Mulele's rebels included members of the Dinga, the Lori, the Nkutshu, the Shilele, the Suku, the Wongo, and the Yanzi.[54] Their recruitment meant that at the end of October the number of fighters had grown to 940, and that by the end of December 1963 it had reached more than 5,000.[55] Women, too, played an important role in the movement. When numbers reached 100,000 at their peak, it was estimated that between 20 and 35% of the partisans were female.[56] As well as the poor, the unemployed, and those who had suffered at the hands of the ANC, unlike other popular revolutions which took place in countries like Cambodia, Mulele's movement did not discriminate against 'intellectuals' such as teachers and office workers, or against traditional enemies of communism such as shop owners and those working for large companies.[57] Finally, as we saw earlier, the movement benefitted from the mutiny of the police in Leopoldville in May 1963.

The training of Mulele's partisans, or Mulelists, was based around two main themes which consisted of explaining to recruits why they were fighting and explaining the ways in which they could fight. Known collectively as Mulelism, the fundaments of Mulele's messages were designed in such a way that they could be easily understood by the rural populations which made up his maquis. Explaining how the white man had colonised the Congo, in which ways the white man's religion had been complicit in their subjugation, and how the inhabitants of Kilamba had been massacred in 1931 after refusing to pay the white man's taxes. After presenting the logic behind the rebellion, the next phase of Mulele's message was to stir the emotions of his listeners and to explain how they could contribute to creating a fairer society. Overtly Marxist in tone, Mulele told his followers how they were now involved in a class struggle between the capitalists who held all the wealth of the Congo in their hands and who benefitted from the labour of the popular masses.[58] Despite all its electoral promises to bring change and to improve the lives of the rural population, Mulele explained that the (Kamitatu) PSA had failed in its mission of providing free medical care, free education and the agricultural machinery necessary to plough and tend the fields. Without these services the children of the masses were unable to gain an education and were unable to aspire to hold important positions in society. The reasons why Kamitatu had failed to do so was that because he was part of a corrupt system under the control of foreigners or imperialists. It was a system comprising security forces, civil employees, businessmen, teachers and missionaries, and these instruments of the state were used to oppress and exploit the masses. While the imperialists and their supporters were the reactionaries who exploited the opportunities offered by the system, Mulele would declare, the partisans were the revolutionary representatives of those in suffering and who lived in poverty. In other terms, he said, the poor were like the dogs which hunted and captured game only for their masters to leave them the bones to feed on.[59]

To fight this oppression and to fight the governors, Mulelists should refuse to obey bad chiefs, soldiers and police, they should refuse to pay taxes and, if necessary, they should do battle with them. Once partisans had destroyed bridges and roads and dismantled the imperialists' system, a new society could be built. Although everyone must show that they were willing to work, the leaders of this regime would provide food and beautiful furnished houses for all. Most importantly, foreigners could not come and steal the wealth of the country. This, partisans were told, was communism.[60]

In as much as the military training was concerned, the partisans' Order Mission was directly inspired by Mao Tse-Tung's Three Main Rules of Discipline and Eight Points for Attention.[61] Designed so that it could be easily understood by the masses, Mulele also designed his rules of combat so that they directly contradicted the behaviour of the ANC troops, and so his partisans would gain the support. Mulele's eight rules, according to his schoolmate Théophile Bula-Bula, were as follows:

- Respect all men, especially the disabled
- Pay villagers an honest price for all goods
- Return everything you borrow
- Replace or pay for anything you damage
- Do not hit or swear at people
- Do not damage or walk on villagers' crop fields
- Do not take liberties with women
- Do not ill-treat captives or steal their possessions[62]

When it came to the question of physical training, the methods used were fairly typical of those found in manuals dealing with insurgency and counterinsurgency. Recruits were taught how to withstand the rain, hunger, thirst and fatigue; they were shown how to move about quickly and undetected by the enemy; they learned hand-to-hand combat, how to kill, how to make, use and maintain weapons.[63] They were taught how they could sabotage bridges and roads in order to stop enemy advances and, to a certain degree, recruits also received training in what could be termed as winning hearts and minds or psychological warfare. This involved carrying out intelligence operations on a local level, distributing propaganda and promoting the revolution throughout villages.[64]

The Organisation of Mulele's Forces

Back in the Kwilu, the battle for who would control the province continued into October 1963: the provincial government continued to crack down on rebel activities and had ordered the ANC to arrest any suspected of aiding Mulele or of being a sympathiser. To counter these measures and to make his forces more effective, on 10 October Mulele decided to carry out a complete structural overhaul.[65] As a whole, the maquis comprised two main groups. Firstly, there were the popular masses and the revolutionary masses which constituted the non-combatant supporters, and secondly, there were the partisans or combatants who would do the actual fighting.[66] Next, with three distinct operational areas being created (around Kalanganda and Bulwem, Iseme and Impasi, and Yassa-Lukwa) Mulele's forces would rely on a four-tier system consisting of a directorate, area commanders, teams of partisans, and village committees.[67] Though it is not known where, exactly, Mulele had his headquarters, or his Central, some sources indicate that they were situated somewhere in the triangle formed by Kikwit, Idiofa and Gungu, and that it was probably around the town of Lukamba.[68]

The directorate of the army was, of course, made up by Mulele and his right-hand-man, Théophile Bengila. Whereas, these two men supervised the political and military activities of the rebel movement as a whole, there were a small number of collaborators who would assist them in the running of operations, particularly when it came to the question of propaganda. Headed by former Josephite Brother Laurentin Ngolo, the role of this department was to draw up documents used in political training, to run the movement's press division, and to keep Mulele aware of developments in Peking, Cuba or Moscow. What it discovered from radio broadcasts, it published in the movement's own magazine, *La voix de la révolution*, or The Voice of the Revolution.[69] In addition providing the movement with its ideological foundations, this first level of the system had more down-to-earth functions. These included providing health care for combatants and their families, stocking the armoury, maintaining discipline through a system of village and military courts. If someone was found guilty of a misdemeanour, the état-major even had a 'prison' where the culprit could be kept. Found within the limits of the compound housing the état-major, the prison was no more than a guarded tent.[70]

The role of second level of the system composed of area commanders was to maintain control of liberated territories. Rising to seven at the height of the rebellion, area commanders would oversee operations carried out in their respective zones and make reports to Mulele, Bengila or Louis Kafungu, the head of the état-major. The third level consisted of teams of partisans typically made up of 53 fighters led by a political and military commissary, and each team contained members responsible for gathering intelligence, for the health of the partisans or for minding their children. As well as these teams, there were village committees led by a chief and the role of each committee was to provide food for rebels and defend the village from attacks. Lastly, the fourth level of the structure composed of high-level commanders' coordinated groups of villages. Often, these commanders had shown that they were the best fighters.[71]

Mulele's Exploitation of Traditional Beliefs and Magic

Though Mulele borrowed and adapted the ideological and military strategies he had acquired in China, his success in inciting the masses to join his revolution lay not only in his ability to apply communist doctrines but also in his ability to exploit the traditional beliefs of the Kwilu's rural population. He was also able to convince his followers that he was endowed with magical powers, and that he could turn arrows into bullets, that he could make himself invisible, that he could turn into a bird, a snake or fly aboard a tiny plane around the forests. This led some supporters to believe that Mulele was all-seeing and ever-present.[72] If the truth be known, Mulele did much to create and perpetuate the myths that surrounded him. One example of how he was able to bewilder his followers came through a trick he had undoubtedly adapted from crowd control methods used by the Force Publique. Whereas soldiers would fire blanks above the heads of people in order to disperse them, Mulele fired blanks at his head to convince his adepts that he was invincible.[73]

In addition to this type of illusion, Mulele would no doubt have been aware of the traditional religious beliefs that were common in the Kwilu. One was that friendly spirits and tribal ancestors possessed the power to rid the Congo of the Europeans,[74] a belief linked to the Mpeve sect who was popular in the 1950s, and another was the belief that sect members could become invisible or invincible merely by imbibing a magical potion. This belief was not limited to the Kwilu, however. In 1961 Mike Hoare witnessed the effects this *dawa* had on Balubakat warriors in northern Katanga. When having swallowed the magic potion, or having smoked hemp, unarmed fighters would run headlong into open fire believing they could not be hurt. The results were those to be expected.

Mulele made sure, then, that each insurgent camp had its own *nganga* (witchdoctor) and that this medicine man had his own concoction ready for consumption. As was the case with the *dawa* in Katanga, this *'Mai Mulele'* (Mulele's water) became ineffective if certain conditions were not respected, or that warriors did not sufficiently believe in the cause.[75] Another form of protection supposedly came through daubing the head and body with a paste made from red clay and carrying amulets containing human fingernails.[76] Another was having a witchdoctor making an incision in a warrior's forehead. A powder being rubbed into the incision was supposed to provide five-day protection from evil but, then again, there were conditions linked to its efficiency. The powder did not work if the warrior washed, if he looked at or frequented women, or if he ate food not prepared by a girl of pre-puberty age.[77] Finally, there were a certain number of other taboos and suspicions that had to be respected. Partisans could only speak Lingala, they could only eat certain parts of an animal, they could not pray, and they could not cut their hair before battle.[78] Such was Mulele's authority and influence over his fighters, it was also believed that if someone broke one of these taboos it would result in them becoming infertile, or making their children susceptible to illness or even death.[79]

From the Beginning to the End of the Kwilu Rebellion

With some sources indicating that the number of partisans reached as many as 90,000-100,000,[80] we could be forgiven for believing that the Kwilu rebellion would be anything other than a resounding success. However, as Mulele was soon to discover, possessing a substantial force and possessing a substantial fighting force are two different things altogether. In effect, an ideological and abstract concept of war can only be won if the physical realities linked to waging that war are present. How, for example, can a war be fought with five FAL rifles, six revolvers, six Sten sub machine guns, three

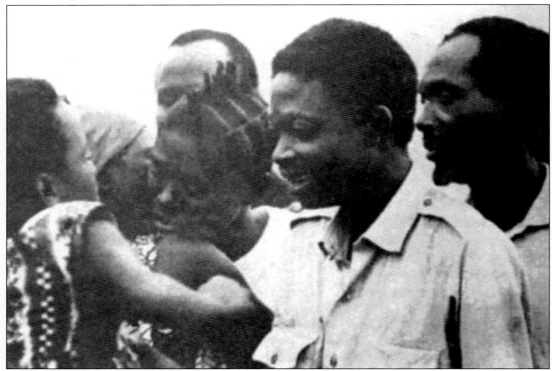

Pierre Mulele on his return to the Congo in 1968. (Courtesy: Babunga.alobi.cd)

Mauser 52s, and four Mauser 36s? These, according to Belgian sources, were the only modern weapons at Mulele's disposal.[81] This tiny armoury being undoubtedly requisitioned by higher-ranking officers and officials, the vast majority of rebels had to make do with bows and arrows, war paint and the belief that swallowing a concoction fashioned by the local witchdoctor would make them invisible. The Kwilu rebellion was destined for failure right from its outset.

It was almost inevitable that the repressive measures used by the ANC and the local gendarmerie from September 1963 would lead to some form of reaction from Mulele and the inhabitants of the Kwilu. Though during the first three months since Mulele began recruitment his partisans carried out small-scale guerrilla-type attacks, blowing up the odd bridge, setting up roadblocks and destroying vehicles was hardly the stuff which made it a full-blown armed revolution. Indeed, nothing more was achieved than the slowing down the advance of government forces into the back of beyond of the province and the capturing of a few weapons. The seeds of rebellion were, nonetheless, being sown.

It was not until 1 January 1964 that Mulele felt that the moment was right to launch a full-scale offensive. Deciding to attack the institutions which underpinned colonialism, the first target for the rebels was the technical school of agriculture in Kikaya in the Bandundu district. As part of the National Institute for Agronomic Study of the Belgian Congo (INEAC), an institute which played an important role in developing the palm oil industry, for Mulele this school was the archetype of Belgian paternalism. Though five European teachers were able to escape and flee to Kikwit, in the attack led by Louis Kafungu a petrol dump containing 60,000 litres of fuel belonging to Lever Brothers was set ablaze.[82] Similarly, a planter working at the INEAC was killed on 5 January and on 8 January an attack on a Portuguese-owned palm oil plant in Lutshima/Madail left nine vehicles destroyed. Whereas the rebels attempted to disrupt policing operations by killing a number of policemen stationed in different outposts in the province, what most shocked observers were the attacks carried out on religious missions. Though Kasa-Vubu had, by then, declared a state of emergency in the Kwilu, and had sent army reinforcements to track down Mulelists, during the night of 22-23 January, three Roman Catholic fathers were slaughtered at Kilembe. Their bodies discovered by nuns in the morning, the priests had been severely beaten and killed with axes and knives. As bridges and roads were blown up and as local officials such as the prefect of Mangai were assassinated, the *jeunesse* gradually invaded other missions to pillage and steal. Though UN helicopters had been deployed to evacuate religious missions at Belo, Intshwem, Lashim, or Matshi, in Mangungu on 26 January an American Baptist missionary named Irene Ferrell was killed by a poison arrow. Seven other Protestant American missionaries were evacuated by Swedish UN forces at Mukedi and at Banda two days earlier, and on 24 January missionaries were robbed of their belongings in Ngoso or in Tshikapa.[83]

Having killed more than 100 policeman, civil servants and territorial agents,[84] a mixture of intimidation and brutality had also seen the rebellion spread from district to district and by the end of February 1964 Mulele's forces controlled a stretch of land 300 kilometres long and 120 kilometres wide.[85]

Though this progress was significant and held the promise of future territorial gains, by mid-March the rebels were starting to lose tempo and were suffering heavy losses in battle. More than 1,000 were killed during an attack on the ANC at Gungu on 7 February, and hundreds more were killed when a renewed attempt to take the garrison was repelled.[86] Partially attributable to the rebels being armed only with assegais, bows and arrows, and partially attributable to a better-performing ANC trained under the auspices of the US Military Assistance Program (MAP), the bulk of casualties were inflicted by the newly-formed Congolese Air Force (Force Aérienne Congolaise, FAC). Flying T-6 Texans armed with .50 calibre machine guns; their anti-Castro Cuban pilots decimated Mulelist concentrations.

These military factors are, of course, crucial to understanding why the intensity of the Kwilu rebellion was so short-lived. A further reason is that Mulele was also beginning to lose the psychological war in the province and was losing popular support. This can be attributed to a famine which forced large numbers of the Kwilu's inhabitants to seek food and shelter offered by the ANC and, secondly, to the huge amounts of casualties. Though the *dawa* supposedly offered protection, when it became clear that it gave none, villagers were deterred from joining the ranks of Mulele's forces. Faced with these shortages, Mulele began forceful recruitment. This acted not as an incentive, but as another reason not to enrol.

Further offensives made by the ANC throughout March and April 1964 and a scorched earth policy implemented to root out rebels meant that by March 1965 barely 2,000 rebels now made up

Mulele's forces.[87] They had continued to mount renewed attacks on Idiofa and they did continue to burn missions in the spring and summer of 1964, however, they had also been forced to retreat and had made no significant ground against ANC incursions. This led Mobutu to believe that victory over the rebels would be certain and that Mulele would soon be arrested and delivered to Leopoldville.[88] Though these predictions may seem slightly optimistic given the fighting capabilities of the ANC, the still dwindling numbers in Mulele's camp saw the Kwilu rebellion come to a grinding halt towards the end of 1965. Mulele had been forced to move camp several times, his second-in-command Thomas Bengila had been banished from the rebellion for impregnating a young village girl and, to cap it all, Kasa-Vubu had identified the rebellion as no longer posing a threat and had lifted the state of emergency.[89]

The Kwilu rebellion came to an end when Mulele decided to seek refuge in the village of Mayili in March 1966 and when the last of his rebel forces were captured or returned to their villages in November 1967. As for Mulele, he firstly went to Brazaville on 2 September 1968 where he attempted to seek political asylum at the Cuban Embassy. Being convinced by the Cubans that he could return safely to Kinshasa (Leopoldville), he was then escorted back to the capital on 29 September by Congolese Minister of Justice, Justin Bomboko. Despite Bomboko's friendly welcome it soon became clear that Mulele would not be treated as a guest and that he would have to face some sort of justice. Imprisoned at Camp Kokolo along with Thomas Bengila on 2 October 1968, the following day both were executed by ANC soldiers in the cruellest fashion imaginable. While still alive, their eyes were pulled out, their genitals ripped off and their arms and legs amputated. What was left was put into a sack and thrown into the Congo River.[90]

7
The Kivu Rebellion

If the Kwilu rebellion was quite limited in terms of the area of land and numbers involved, the rebellion which took place in the eastern and northern provinces in 1964 was far greater in scale. In the end the Kwilu rebellion did not achieve its objectives: it did not lead to any major change in Leopoldville; it failed to gain the support of the popular masses it required; it failed to increase support of different tribes; it failed to tempt the communist bloc into providing assistance; and it failed to overcome even the most disorganised of national armies. The Eastern rebellion – sometimes referred to as the 'Simba rebellion' – was a different beast altogether. Though there are a number of similarities with events which took place in the Kwilu, and there are tenuous links between Mulele and the leaders of the eastern rebellion, we should understand that the latter accomplished just about everything that the former did not: its support was not ethnically limited and it was supported by the communist bloc politically as well as militarily. Some observers have even suggested that the eastern rebellion was more like a revolution in that Adoula's government was overthrown, albeit peacefully, and the vast majority of people supported the revolution in the areas affected.[1]

The Origins of the Kivu Rebellion

As we saw in the previous chapter, the conditions which ignited popular unrest in eastern Congo were related to the sense that independence had brought little significant change in the fortunes of the country's rural population due to the perceptions that one political elite had simply been replaced by another, and that despite the promises the inhabitants of rural areas had been more or less neglected. Indeed, little had been done to raise the living standards of the poorest, political corruption was widespread, the ANC seemed to be merely an instrument used to control and abuse the rural population, and with the virtual disappearance of local political movements and elections the inhabitants of provinces such as Maniema, North Kivu and Central Kivu found themselves denuded of the means to mount any political opposition to the elite.[2] As was the case in the Kwilu, the conditions were perfect for some form of mass protest and for mass armed protest. Effectively, the ANC remained as inept as ever, though UN peacekeepers which had been in the Congo since August 1960 were gradually being withdrawn. This was an important factor as the UNOC's 20,000 peacekeepers had been the only force that had shown it was capable of maintaining some semblance of public order. UNOC's mission in the Congo ended in June 1964.

To understand how popular dissatisfaction transmuted into full-blown rebellion we first of all need to return to September 1963 and to the events which led to the creation of the so-called National Council for Liberation (Conseil National de Libération, CNL). We

APL leaders (left to right): Colonel Kandeka, Christophe Gbenye, Gaston Soumaliot, and Nicolas Olenga.

Gaston Soumaliot flanked by Pierre Mulele and Gaston Soumaliot.

will remind ourselves that on a political level a split in the PSA had led to the anti-government Gizenga wing opposing the pro-government Norbert Leta wing in the Kwilu. In order to crack down on anti-government political activities in the province, Leta had used his legislative powers to arrest prominent PSA-G representatives. One example is the arrest of Marc Katshunga, the leader of the party's central committee in Kikwit on 23 September 1963. His detention coincided with that of Antoine Gizenga who continued to be held on the island prison of Bula-Bemba on the Congo River. In protest against Gizenga's incarceration several members of the PSA-G organised a demonstration in the national parliament in Leopoldville on 25 September. Criticising the government's links to the pro-west Binza Group over the course of the coming parliamentary sessions, the PSA-G managed to gain the support of representatives from the MNC-L, and two smaller Congolese political parties, the Parti Nationale de la Convention du Peuple (PNCP), and the Union Démocratique Africaine (UDA). Four days later, and with no end to protests in sight, President Kasa-Vubu took the decision to dissolve parliament and signed orders forbidding the activities of nationalist parties. This was decision which was to provoke uproar and the government's opponents now found themselves deprived of any means of mounting legislative resistance in the Congolese parliament. A day later, on 30 September, representatives including Christophe Gbenye, Egide Bocheley-Davidson, and Gabriel Yumbu took the decision to set up the CNL.[3] They did so two days later in Brazaville in the Republic of the Congo. This was due not only to the proximity of the city but also because the moderate Fulbert Youlou had been replaced by the radical Alphonse Massamba-Débat, an advocate of 'scientific socialism' and anti-colonialism. The CNL issued its *Manifeste de lancement*, or 'Starting Manifesto' on 3 October in which it presented its plans to implement a political programme which would see the total decolonisation of the Congo and freedom from the influence of foreign powers. Clearly identifying the United States through its reference to 'yankee oppression', criticism was also directed at Kasa-Vubu's government which it saw as characterised by 'fascism, the abuse of power and fraud'.[4] The manifesto called for an end to all the institutions set up within the parameters of the *Loi fondamentale* (1960), i.e. President, Parliament, and government, and declared that Congo free elections should be held and that a parliament for all the people be elected.[5] Though its intentions were sincere, the CNL was riven by internal dispute. This stemmed mostly from Christophe Gbenye of the MNC-L being elected to lead the group and some members doubting his radical credentials and his political commitment. Indeed, it was Gbenye who had signed Gizenga's arrest warrant in January 1962.[6] Eventually this political infighting between the PSA-G and the MNC-L resulted in the CNL splitting into two in February 1964 and, as is often the case when one group splits, two new groups were created. Gbenye, who had been expelled from the group, created the CNL-G; while on the other side of the division Bocheley-Davidson set up the CNL-B. In spite of their having very similar political objectives, how to achieve these objectives led to them adopting different strategies on how to overthrow Kasa-Vubu.[7] On the one hand, Bocheley-Davidson preferred a more ideological approach to revolution, whereas Gbenye opted for armed struggle and the opening up of a new military front in the east.[8] From the Kwilu where he had offered support to Mulele, he subsequently sent two of his military commanders to Northern Katanga and to the Kivu province respectively.[9]

The Organisation of the Simba Forces
As well as the social conditions already mentioned above, still significant political support for the MNC in the eastern Congo meant that the region was an ideal place in which Gbenye could drum up support and form a militia. The first steps Gbenye took to doing so came with the appointment of Gaston Soumialot and Laurent Kabila to coordinate activities in the Kindu and Northern Katanga respectively. Soumialot was an avowed Lumumbist who had been sent by the CNL to Bujumbura in early 1964 to receive training from the Chinese and during his time in Burundi he had Congolese nationalists such as Fuliiru[10] leaders Louis Bidalira and Musa Marandura.[11] He also met the leader of the Bembe people, Jerôme Mutshangu and received support from Rwandan Tutsi refugees of the Rwandan National Union (UNAR).[12] This would prove to be a significant encounter as we shall see later. As for Kabila, a man described by Che Guevara as realising perfectly well that the 'main enemy was North American imperialism',[13] he had also been a member of the CNL. In May 1964 with the help of youths from the Holoholo tribe Kabila organised a coup against Jason Sendwe.[14]

His alliance with this tribe residing mainly around what was then Albertville would also prove decisive. With their tribal brethren living on the opposite side of Lake Tanganyika, we can postulate that this tribal link played an important role when arms were being transferred across the lake from Tanzania. From a military point of view, Gbenye appointed Nicolas Olenga. Eventually becoming a 'general' in the army officially known as the Armée Populaire de Libération (APL), Olenga was a former railway clerk who had

RIPE FOR REBELLION: POLITICAL AND MILITARY INSURGENCY IN THE CONGO, 1946-1964

Ernesto Che Guevara (left side of the photo) in one of the Simba camps in the eastern Congo in 1964.

Some of the early Simba warriors could be described as a mix of ANC-defectors and tribal fighters. Certainly enough, they wore a suitable mix of uniforms and personal decorations – but were poorly led, armed, and ill-disciplined.

Laurent Kabila, while acting a Simba ambassador to Nairobi, in Kenya. This small-time revolutionary of the mid-1960s, subsequently 'converted' himself into a successful businessman. Ultimately, he was to return to the Congo in 1996, lead the Rwandan (and US-supported) invasion, and then rule the country from 1997 until 2001.

learned the rudiments of revolutionary warfare when part of Antoine Gizenga's Stanleyville government in 1961.[15] As was the case with the majority of those that joined rebel forces and became 'Simba' or 'lions', Olenga knew very little about communist ideology. The Simba were simply tribesmen looking to take material and physical advantage of a chaotic situation. In similar circumstances to those seen in the Kwilu, but on a far larger scale, the contribution of the Simba aged mainly between 12 and 20 years old consisted largely in raping any girl or woman they could lay their hands on while wearing a variety of clothing including animal skins and leaves from banana plants. Later on in their campaign, having ransacked the homes of European settlers, many would take to wearing women's dresses and underwear. Some even took to wearing lampshades as hats. In part, this can be explained by their also taking a *dawa*, smoking hemp, and drinking any alcohol captured during their raids.

The Advance of the Simba

The first signs of any serious disorder occurred on 15 April 1964 when the Simba attacked police stations in Bukavu on the southern tip of Lake Kivu.[16] Killing 42 people, the next targets were also police stations in Luvungi, Lemera, Mulenge and Kiliba.[17] From there, using firearms and brandishing hand-written signs strangely demonstrating a loyalty to Pierre Mulele, as many as 5,000 warriors – said to have links with the Kabare people – made their way to Bukavu. Though they had virtually no modern weapons except for those captured from the ANC the Simba made rapid progress and within two months the APL was in control of North Katanga, Maniema, Sankuru, all of the eastern provinces and parts of the Equateur province in the north west of the country. Highly motivated and believing themselves to be impervious to enemy bullets, they frightened the ANC soldiers who, tribesmen themselves, also believed in the power of magical potions. After victory had been won over the ANC in one town, on certain occasions all the CNL had to do was to send a telegraph to those in the next town to tell them of the Simba's coming arrival. Entire garrisons of government troops would be deserted in fear, and in the ensuing panic to escape from the Simba, the ANC would abandon its weapons and leave them for the rebels to pick up.[18] Before long, with virtually no resistance to their advance being offered, the Simba

Two more Simba warriors wearing a mix of civilian and military clothes and traditional tribal decorations.

ANC soldiers often defected and joined the Simba.

had reached larger towns such as Uvira, Fizi and Baraka,[19] situated on the southern and northern banks of Lake Tanganyika. Such was their strength in numbers with some ANC having joined their ranks, the next stage in Olenga's strategy was to take Stanleyville in the Oriente province. This stronghold of Lumumbism and the Congo's third largest city was considered as a major symbolic objective due to its link to the defunct prime minister and due to Gizenga's failed attempt to set up a breakaway government some three and a half years earlier.

To Stanleyville

Life on the whole was pretty good for the inhabitants of Stanleyville. Situated on the banks of the River Congo some 140 miles south of the Central African Republic and some 140 miles west of Uganda, in 1964 Stanleyville's population of around 150,000 people could enjoy the shops situated along Avenue Prince Charles, Avenue Princesse Marie-José or Avenue de l'Eglise. They could take a walk along the promenade, watch films being shown at the Palace Cinema, swim in the pool that bore the name Leopold III, or they could dine in one of Stanleyville's restaurants like the 'Pourqoui Pas'. There were schools, an airport, hotels, hospitals and, of course, there were luxurious houses. These could be found on delightfully named streets such as the Avenue des Eucalyptus, the Avenue des Erables (maple) or the Avenue des Cocotiers (coconut trees); their names reflecting the type of fauna that could be found on the arable lands surrounding the city. It should be said that when we say 'the' inhabitants, we are, naturally, referring mainly to the Europeans that had emigrated to, or were stationed in, the city and who operated the Philips Radio shop, the Comptoir Belgika to trade in diamonds, palm oil, coffee and rubber. We could also be referring to the *évolués*. They, too, could be found working as clerks in the Standard Bank,

Many of the Simbas could only be described as 'child soldiers'.

A group of Simbas during their advance on Stanleyville.

Until 1964, the life and scenery in downtown Stanleyville was closely reminiscent of that in many West European cities.

or in any number of businesses that employed the literate and the French-speaking. For the majority, i.e. the native Congolese, they would have to put up with jobs as porters, kitchen maids or as servers in restaurants or domestics in private houses. It should come as no surprise, then, that they venerated Patrice Lumumba and the MNC. Seen as a martyr of the struggle to bring equal rights to the Congolese, there is now a memorial to Lumumba in Kisangani, the current-day name of Stanleyville. Neither should it come as a surprise when we consider that Antoine Gizenga chose the city as his base. A leading member of the PSA, it was somehow straightforward that Olenga would choose to follow in his footsteps.

He did so in early August 1964 after the Simba had taken the city of Kindu in the Maniema province some 250 miles south of Stanleyville. Heading northwards in trucks captured from the ANC, the first reports that Olenga's troops were approaching Stanleyville came on 2 August when they arrived in Wanie Rukula, a village only 24 miles away.[20] Being guarded by companies of ANC stationed at either Camp Sergeant Ketele, Camp Prince Charles or at Camp Leopold II, and with paracommandos being flown in from Leopoldville, we could wonder that there might be some resistance to Olenga's advance and that Stanleyville's foreign population would be protected. Moreover, only a short time before, Soumialot had broadcast a radio message assuring foreigners that they would not meet any harm. They were needed, and they would be happier than under the Leopoldville regime, promised the rebel leader.[21]

Just as a precaution, several hundred Europeans and their families were evacuated over the next few days. This was fortunate as on 6 August the Simba had reached Stanleyville's Simi-Simi Airport and were now shooting at planes attempting to land. Indeed, a US C-47 carrying Colonel Leonard Mulumba, the commander of ANC forces in Stanleyville was forced to withdraw under enemy fire.[22] Despite these hurried evacuations around 1,600 foreign nationals remained in Stanleyville. Loathe to leave businesses and shops they had set up and preferring to weather the coming storm, many of them had been had been in Stanleyville since after the Second World War when the Belgian government encouraged them to settle in the Congo. They had survived the beatings they had been dealt when Gizenga took over the city in 1960-1961 so why should they leave now. The reason why Belgians, Greeks, Italians and a number of

Pakistanis should have filled the empty seats of the rescue planes was to become very clear over the next 16 weeks or so.

The first signs that the Simba had entered Stanleyville came a little time after the C-47 had withdrawn. Looking down from the window of the US consulate situated on Avenue Eisenhower, Consul Michael Hoyt and vice-consul David Grinwiss saw ANC troops firing wildly at Camp Ketele. This was ominous as it indicated that the Simba now occupied the buildings.[23] Hoyt became more worried when the firing stopped and the Simba now came towards the consulate. Led by a sorcerer waving a palm branch, a single file of seven or eight Simba followed behind and walked along Avenue Eisenhower. Naked to the waist and unarmed, the presence of the ANC was nowhere to be seen: frightened to death by the spectacle, they simply lay down their weapons and either fled or surrendered. Some were executed on the spot, and some were tortured to death.[24] The attack on the US consulate followed a short time later. On hearing the shots outside the consulate Hoyt and his staff decided the best place to seek refuge was in the security vault. It had an inner door made of steel and could be locked from the inside. Despite efforts to break down the door of the vault with rifle butts, for the time being the five Americans hiding in the vault were safe.

As US officials in Washington attempted to rescue the consulate staff through the abandoned Operation Flagpole, the mood of the Simba in Stanleyville was beginning to change for the worse. Though not directly menacing the lives of Europeans at this stage, the Simba were, however, pilfering businesses and houses and making threats as they sought out ANC troops. The reason why the mood had changed was that Olenga had arrived in Stanleyville. Six feet tall, with a goatee beard and a moustache, Olenga carried himself like an officer even though he had never received military training. Having acquired an oversized khaki-coloured uniform, it boasted three stars, gold braid and a piece of leopard skin.[25] After visiting his army at Camp Ketele, the first meeting on Olenga's agenda was to meet Belgian consul Patrick Nothomb. Affirming to Nothomb that he was pleased there were no Belgian or English mercenaries fighting his rebels, bizarrely the target of his verbal attack was the United States. Olenga claimed that American regular soldiers were fighting in the Congo, and even more strangely claimed that the Simba had killed over 200 of them. The state of Olenga's delusions reached a height when he later claimed that Belgium had dropped an atomic bomb on a Congolese town. According to him, it had killed over 10,000 people.[26]

Until 11 August Stanleyville remained relatively calm by Simba standards. However, it should not be understood that the lives of Europeans in Stanleyville were not in danger or that there were no exactions carried out against them, or other foreign nationals: the five Americans were arrested and sentenced to death as were all Belgians, Catholic priests, and Protestants in other parts of rebel-held areas.[27]

Political Developments: The Return of Moïse Tshombe

It would be fair to say that Prime Minister Cyrille Adoula had been given plenty of time to take the Congolese situation from one of disorderly to orderly. However, despite tens of millions of dollars being provided in funds to give advice to tribal leaders, to buy the allegiance of army officers, to assist parliamentary manoeuvring, to set up radio broadcasts, newspapers, to maintain good relations with union leaders, and to influence UN delegates, since Adoula's becoming premier in August 1961, the Congo had witnessed a quasi-permanent state of war between one warring faction or another. When we look to point a finger at those responsible for the creation of such chaos, however, we should not only point to Adoula. By the end of May 1964, for example, US analysts saw Mobutu as partly to blame, putting the 'ineffectiveness and disarray' of the ANC down to his 'vanity and irresponsibility'.[28] Moreover, with the performances of the Congo's security forces going from bad to worse and their being routed by Pygmies in the Kivu in June 1964, the unfortunate fact was both the military and political situations were confused. The government was weak, political unrest was on the increase, the army was unreliable and the insurgency was spreading. It was feared that if the rebels took Bakavu, then there may well be a serious political crisis in Leopoldville and fighting in other cities such as Stanleyville.[29] As we have just seen, both these predictions made by the US State Department were to become a frightening reality. Running out of alternatives at this time and fearing further communist infiltration, US government agencies were examining options that would provide a boost to Adoula's regime. As the option of sending US troops into the Congo had been ruled out as US military commitments in Vietnam were steadily increasing, the United States Information Agency (USIA) even stepped up its level of psywar operations. Indeed, in early July, USIA director Carl Rowan dispatched John W. Mowinckel to set up Radio Congo. Its objective was to broadcast psychological information to listeners in the Congo, and was part of a larger US psywar programme which would cover Africa.[30] Finally, in view of his anti-Communist convictions, State officials in Washington decided to sound out Moïse Tshombe who, at this time, was still in Madrid. If Tshombe did decide to return to the Congo, it was hoped that it would be done 'legally' (i.e. peacefully) and that his return did not amount to a coup d'état using Katangese gendarmes as the means to mount it.[31]

As the last of the UN peacekeepers left the Congo towards the end of June 1964, the US Joint Strategic Survey Council (JSSC) began to take a grave view of a context which was rapidly deteriorating. In a memorandum to the Joints Chiefs of Staff dated 25 June 1964, the council (sometimes committee) pointed out that the CNL had received financial

Moise Tshombe with US Ambassador McMurtrie Godley.

assistance from the USSR and from the PRC, and that Chinese and Czech agents were providing intelligence to rebel forces in the east from their bases in Burundi. Suggesting that Adoula's 'moderate coalition' had failed and that the Congo's situation was 'unpromising', the council believed also believed it was time for strongman politics in Leopoldville and that the only person fitting that description was Tshombe. To add to these credentials, Tshombe was a 'creature' created by UMHK, he was pro-West, he commanded loyalty, and the chances were that he could firstly establish control of Katanga before gaining control of the rest of the country. While the United States had reservations about giving support to a man so closely linked to Belgian colonialism, it believed that if it did nothing the DRC would disintegrate and become a communist-controlled entity. The best option for the United States, according to the JSSC, was to persuade President Kasa-Vubu to appoint Tshombe as prime minister. After Kasa-Vubu had done so, the US 'should give strong and overt political support to Tshombe as the legal government'.[32] With such heavy political backing from the US, it is no wonder that the very next day Tshombe had left exile in Spain and returned to Leopoldville at the behest of both Kasa-Vubu and Adoula. Though there was initial speculation as to just exactly what role Tshombe would perform, by 11 July Kasa-Vubu had dismissed Adoula and had named Tshombe to replace him. Kasa-Vubu's ability to make such unilateral decisions came via a national referendum held the day before. From now on, the cabinet was responsible to the president rather than to Parliament.

Tshombe wasted little time in setting up his own government. Gone was Adoula's team of ineffectual ministers, and in came fellow Katangan Godefroid Munongo as Minister of the Interior. Immediately after settling into office, Tshombe began to plan the reconquest of the Congo and its liberation from Mulele's rebels in the Kwilu and Soumialot's rebels in eastern Congo. He called on US Ambassador McMurtrie Godley to complain of breakdowns of the Makasi T-28s and declared that he would be repatriating a force of 4,000 Katangese gendarmes from Angola. His objective – one approved by Mobutu who was present at the meeting – was to restore order in North Katanga and retake the provincial capital.[33] Albertville, as we have seen, had fallen to rebel soldiers on 19 June.

8
Counter-insurrection in the Congo, 1964

As the ragtag army of Simba warriors marched into Stanleyville on 6 August, plans were already under way to prevent the Congo from falling into total collapse. With no effective internal security force in place and no external help in prospect, it was believed that Elisabethville and Leopoldville would soon be under rebel control.[1] Bearing in mind, the consensus of opinion surrounding the ANC, one if the first measures to be envisaged by US officials was that an emergency force officered by Belgians already present in the Congo should take command of the national army. Then, if Belgian Foreign Minister Paul-Henri Spaak agreed to this proposal, this force would be supplemented by a mercenary gendarmerie.[2] Though Spaak initially refused to authorise Belgian military support, it would appear with his subsequent approval that his decision was swayed by events taking place concurrently in Stanleyville. The rebel capture of Stanleyville had, indeed, been a turning point in the insurrection in many respects. Purely from a psychological point of view, the CNL could now boast that it controlled one of the largest cities in the Congo as well as much of the Kivu, Maniema, areas of Katanga, and areas of Kasai. The CNL could exploit these successes and, with growing popular support, could envisage further advances into government held territory.

Though Colonels Williams and Dodds of the US Mission in the Congo (COMISH) expressed the view that a force of mercenaries did not guarantee success, to all intents and purposes, Tshombe had already designed plans to revert to the use of some sort of foreign legion in the Congo. Just a few days after being appointed prime minister, on 11 July his Katangese gendarmes of the Forces Katangaises Libres (FKL) had marched over the border from Angola.[3] Many would serve in the French-speaking mercenary units of 9 and 10 Commandos led by Belgian Lieutenant Charles Gardien and by Lt-Colonel Jean Schramme respectively. Known also as the Bataillon Léopard, this unit operated mainly in the northern areas of the Congo alongside 6 Commando, another French-speaking unit commanded by Robert 'Bob' Denard. Whereas these commandos

Bob Denard.

were relatively small and acted quasi-independently, a much larger mercenary force commanded by Mike Hoare had been in the process of being put together as early as the end of July. A veteran of the Katangan campaign and a friend of Tshombe, Hoare now met the Congolese leader, Munongo and Mobutu at the Memling Hotel in Leopoldville. Listening to Mobutu's plans to recapture Manono, Albertville, Fizi, and Uvira, the ANC's chief of staff estimated that he would need a mercenary force of some 1,000 men. Acting in

Members of 6 Commando with Bob Denard (centre).

conjunction with ANC forces would be required for an attack on Stanleyville.[4]

Using methods very similar to those used to recruit the Compagnie Internationale and 4 Commando in 1961, adverts were placed in newspapers such as the *Johannesburg Star* and called for 'any fit young man looking for employment with a difference'.[5] The salary offered inside a unit known as 5 Commando was £150 per month, plus £5 per day extra if in combat, and an additional £2 per day spent in an 'Insecurity Zone'.[6] A similar recruiting campaign was led in Rhodesia where men were recruited in Salisbury (now Harare) to serve with 'special white units' of the Congolese National Army. *The Times* (London) reported that the recruits would be flown to Kamina Air Base by a Rhodesian commercial airline. On board a Rhodesia Air Services (RAS) Skymaster that flew to the Congo via Jan Smuts airport some days later were 36 South Africans, Rhodesians, Italians, Belgians and Germans. They had been told by recruiters that the 'old idea' of having European officers and black foot soldiers did not work as the 'blacks were only too willing to retreat in sticky places'. As such, the 'new idea' was to form all white units of men.
[7] *The New York Times* reported that while recruitment in South Africa was carried out by Major Jacques C. Puren (sic),[8] Alistair Wicks, a former pilot with Rhodesian Air Services was responsible for recruitment in Rhodesia.[9] Another report in *The Times* of 24 August spoke of how a group of 30 Belgians and Frenchmen had arrived in Léopoldville on a flight from Brussels and how a South African Air Force (SAAF) C-130 transport aircraft had also been used to bring in mercenaries.[10] Aboard these flights were men such as Regimental Sergeant-Major Arthur Lindsay (Jack) Carton-Barber and 5 Commando's future commander John Peters. Never numbering more than 300 men at any given time,[11] 5 Commando was divided up into units comprising 30-40 men known as 51, 52, 53, 54, 55, 56, 57, and 58 Commandos. Though all of these units were under the overall command of Hoare, they each had an individual commander. Among the leaders were:

- 51 Commando led by former British Army Lieutenant Gary Wilson
- 52 Commando led by former SS Captain Siegfried Meueller
- 53 Commando led by South African Lt. Jack Maiden
- 58 Commando led by CIA officer William 'Rip' Robertson.

A veteran of CIA covert operations in Guatemala and at the Bay of Pigs, Robertson led a group of anti-Castro Cubans who had initially been sent to the Congo to rescue the American hostages in Stanleyville. Codenamed Low Beam, this operation was abandoned as it was feared that any small-scale approach on the city made by land or river would be detected and that local inhabitants would alert rebel forces by using jungle drums.[12] This explains, in part, why a much larger ground force provided with air support from other Cuban exiles would be used to reconquer eastern Congo before marching on Stanleyville. All these forces were involved in an operation known as the Ommegang. This term of Flemish origin originally used to describe a form of religious procession, if the attacks made on religious missions can be considered as attacks on one of the foundations of Western civilisation, then the Ommegang – whose role was to destroy the Simba and their communist backers – was probably considered by its conceiver as a form of Christian crusade.

The Ommegang

As operation Low Beam was abandoned and as US state officials baulked at the idea of involving the Organisation of African Unity (OAU) to negotiate the release of American hostages,[13] they gradually became resigned to

Troops of 1 Commando with a M3 White scout car wearing the insignia of that unit.

the fact that they would have to give their full support to military operations involving South African mercenaries. Indeed, if any cooperation with what was fast becoming considered in international circles as a rogue state was discovered, it was feared that it would create an adverse reaction among the US public and jeopardise

5 Commando's Mike Hoare (standing centre) with John Peters (crouching) in front of a Bell-47 of the Congolese Air Force.(Photo by Bob Houke)

Members of 6 Commando at Bouta. The Bell-47 bears the logo of the Makasi. (Photo by Bob Houke)

'general African policies and programs'.[14] In the event, Tshombe was equally suspicious of the OAU and had expelled the nationals from the member states of Congo-Brazzaville, Mali, and Burundi for alleged subversive activities. In addition, at an extraordinary session of the OAU held in Addis Ababa on 5 September 1964 it was agreed that Jomo Kenyatta of Kenya should head a special conciliatory commission in the Congo. Tshombe's suspicions surrounding OAU motives were confirmed when Kenyatta called for a ceasefire and an end to Belgian and American support for Tshombe.[15]

While US officials and Moïse Tshombe attempted to diffuse a potentially damaging diplomatic minefield, a group of Belgian officers commissioned by Tshombe in the aftermath of his appointment were also trying to devise plans to garner foreign support for the rescue of their fellow countrymen and women in Stanleyville and in the surrounding areas. Aware that the Belgian Foreign Minister had shown a degree of reticence when it came to committing military assistance, they explained to Spaak how he could be of help in a matter of 'exceptional seriousness'.[16] This plan conceived by Colonels Vandewalle, Guillaume Logiest and Louis Marlière was as follows:

1) The role of the Commander-in-chief should be eased by providing him with a special headquarters from which he can direct operations to re-establish order. These headquarters should be entrusted to a military advisor to the Commander-in-chief who would, in turn, be assisted by a small number of Congolese advisors and officers in charge of their own sections.

2) A 'small packet' policy should be avoided at all costs: a fire cannot be put out by throwing cups of water at it. What is needed is a plan whose results can only be seen in several weeks' time.

3) A reserve made up of the best available troops (ex-Katanganese Gendarmes) must be put in place. This reserve which will receive intensive training has to be stationed in the zone where offensives moving to the north will start. At least ten companies of soldiers are needed.

4) Using this reserve, its airborne support, foreign volunteers and technicians, offensives will be carried out according to a plan drawn up by the operational headquarters and the Commander-in-chief.

5) Foreign volunteers should be 'handled solidly' (sic).

6) [...] It is impossible to hope to turn around a situation as serious as this in 24 or 48 hours. We should take advantage of the next fortnight to prepare the offensive which will bring certain success. Airfields, road and train hubs will be the principal objectives. The rest [of the Congo]

Ferret scout car used by 6 Commando at Bouta. (Photo by Bob Houke)

Table 3: Composition of the 5th Mechanised Brigade	
Lima 1	Lima 2
300 mercenaries (5 Commando's seven companies plus Cuban commandos).	One armoured unit
Belgian regular forces.	350 Baluba tribesmen.
300 ANC.	8 Commando (logistics team and three infantry companies under the command of Lieutenant-Colonel Lamouline).
7 Commando (logistics team, three infantry companies).	9 Commando or Force Papa (logistics team, an infantry company and a battalion of ANC commanded by Major Protin).
A unit made up of Balemba tribesmen.	10 Commando led by Jean Schramme.
6 Commando led by Bob Denard (six platoons numbered 61 to 65 and a platoon of paratroopers commanded by Lieutenant Topor).	

does not matter. Léopoldville and Haut-Katanga must be held at all cost as well as communication links between Léo[poldville] and E'ville.' [17]

After the feasibility of implementing these plans had been examined, on 24 August Spaak signed the Ministerial Order giving Vandewalle the authorisation to lead the mission in the Congo. This was quickly followed on 28 August by an order signed by General Mobutu and Tshombe which gave Vandewalle the responsibility of coordinating ground and airborne operations.[18] The question of ways put in place, Vandewalle now turned his attention to the means with which the Ommegang could be executed effectively.[19] From a general point of view, the plan drawn up by Vandewalle called for the division of the Congo into four parts in which different battalions of a larger unit called the 5th Mechanised Brigade would operate:

- Group One (51 Commando) would be responsible for the area which comprised Luluabourg;
- Group Two (52 Commando) for a large portion of western Congo which included Léopoldville, Coquilhatville and Lisala in the north-west;
- Group Three (53 Commando) in the area covering territory between Bukavu and Bunia; and
- Group Four (54 Commando) which would operate in the area north of Elisabethville.

The forces used in these operations would be two groups of three battalions which would become operational before 15 October and 15 November respectively. The objectives of the plan were to retake the Kivu by 30 October using three battalions, and to gain control of Stanleyville by 15 December.[20] The four groups were then divided in two and were given the names Lima 1 and Lima 2. They were supplied with equipment from the United States[21] and commanded more than 150 trucks, armoured cars and jeeps.[22] Both groups were to be supplied with air cover provided by the Makasi pilots.

Inasmuch as the actual advance on Stanleyville, all the forces were to assemble at Kamina, Katanga in mid-September 1964. From here, elements of Vandewalle's 5th Mechanised Brigade[23] would retake Kabalo in northern Katanga in order to clear the path for the advance on Stanleyville. Concurrently, companies of 5 Commando would be flown to different areas of the Congo in order to put down any threat of a counterattack by rebel forces, and to make their way to Stanleyville. 51 Commando under British Lieutenant Gary Wilson was to be transported to Coquilhatville and then on to Gamena further north where they joined a column headed by Major Genisse. Here, they were also joined by nine men from 'Rip' Robertson's 58 Commando, units from Bob Denard's 6 Commando, and a company of the ANC. With the objective of this column being to reach Paulis in the north-east of the Congo before making its way to Stanleyville, after Bumba had been taken, 51 Commando and Robertson's men would be flown to Kindu to join the spearhead column. In the meantime, 52 Commando under Captain Siegfried Meueller[24] also flew to Coquilhatville to join a column led by Major Lemercier which also included 10 Commando, units of the ANC,

5 Commando seen after the capture of Stanleyville. (via author)

would be shot first in the feet, then the shins, knees, thighs and the head.[30]

Sixty miles to the east of Coquilhatville on 10 September 1964, mercenary forces under the command of Mueller attacked Ingende, where they defeated rebel forces, and then marched on Boende. In this town on the River Tshuapa, one member of 52 Commando was killed and four were wounded. Withdrawing to Bikili, 52 Commando successfully repulsed an attack by enemy forces. Volunteer Nel was killed.[31] Despite this success under the leadership of Mueller, on 12 October 24 South African mercenaries mutinied against his leadership accusing Mueller of 'incompetence', being 'too soft', and of being indecisive in combat'.[32] Mueller would shortly be replaced by Lt. Ben Louw.

Joining Colonel Mulamba's ANC unit the role of 52 Commando was to attack rebel forces around Uvira, Lubero and Butembo before consolidating its positions in the Great Lakes region.[33] On 7 October, it was reported that 40 'South African' mercenaries and 20 Congolese troops captured the lakeside town of Uvira. In what was considered the Congolese Government's biggest victory since the beginning of the rebellion five months previously, 53 Commando cut off the road to Bujumbura. Reaching Uvira, 30 Europeans, (mainly Italians) were rescued and evacuated by USAF transport aircraft.[34] Previous successes for 53 Commando at Bukavu and Kabare led to Hoare describing 53 Commando as 'some of the best material we had at Kamina'. Unsurprisingly given this view, on 28 October, this unit took Butembo and was ordered to wait here until it received orders to move forward with the Stan Column. This spearhead of the advance on Stanleyville left Kongolo on 1 November 1964.[35]

and 54 Commando. These forces would make their way eastwards where they would march on Ingende, Bikili, Boende and Ikela. From here, 52 Commando would join up with Major Genisse's column in Bikili while 54 Commando continued onto Opala and then onto Stanleyville. As for 53 Commando, and the remainder of Robertson's forces, they would be flown to Uvira on Lake Tanganyika before making their way northwards to Bakavu, Goma and Beni. From here, they would march on Mambasa before joining in with attack on Stanleyville. 53 Commando was led by South African Lt. Jack Maiden who was seconded by George Schroeder from Durban.[25] After the liberation of Bukavu, the contingent of nine Cuban commandos who had taken part in the attack would then join up with Robertson's unit and what was called the 'Stan Column' in Kindu. This column which was to spearhead the attack on Stanleyville had been flown in to Kongolo on 31 October 1964 before advancing northwards to Kibombo, Kindu, Punia and Lubutu. From here, they would advance on Stanleyville. With military command of the Column given to Hoare, 55, 56 and 57 Commando (commanded by British Captain Ian Gordon) joined up with the Cuban Exile ground forces.[26]

Despite still undergoing training, 51 Commando was sent from N'djili to Gemena to support the ANC. In early September 1964 these forces attacked and easily defeated over 1,000 enemy soldiers armed with machine guns and bazookas at Lisala, a key Congo River port some 350 miles from Stanleyville. With ANC units in support, 51 Commando found witch doctors hopping up and down holding palm fronds, and rebels wearing khaki camouflage and monkey skins. Armed with only automatic rifles, Wilson's men walked slowly up the hill on which the rebels were situated and fired as they went. With the rebels in the open and with no fear of death, according to Wilson, the ensuing battle was like a 'shooting gallery'. Killing at least 13 rebels, in all 160 enemy soldiers were killed at Lisala.[27] This enabled Hoare's forces to conclude that the enemy was 'greatly overrated' and that the ANC would fight if 'properly led'.[28] Writing in the *New York Times Magazine* two months later, Lloyd Garrison describes Lisala as the 'perfect illustration of why the mercenaries have been imported'.[29] Shortly before the end of October, 51 Commando mercenaries including Rhodesians Roy Whitehead, 'Butch' Schoerman and Joe Wepener; 'Mike', an ex-lawyer from Nairobi; and Barry Hobbins from Canada, moved on to Aketi, and Bumba. In Bumba, a town also situated on the Congo River, the group of mercenaries described as the most consistently successful of all the commandos demonstrated their brutality in shooting six rebel prisoners, justifying this act by saying that the ANC would use far more cruel methods. Indeed, rebel prisoners

The Evolution of Rescue Operations

As mercenary forces made their way into areas under rebel control in September and October the situation for the hostages being held by the Simba took on a far more dramatic dimension. Though, up to that point the rebels believed that they had secured Stanleyville, intelligence services in Leopoldville intercepted a message sent by Simba commander Colonel Opepe to Olenga. It requested permission to execute a certain number of Europeans and Americans held in the city.[36] On receiving news of this request, the Congolese government made a humanitarian appeal to the rebels declaring that killing any hostages would be a 'shocking violation of the Geneva Convention', and an act that 'would constitute a shameful stain on the national honor of the Congolese people'.[37] American authorities also reacted to the message. In a memorandum to W. Averell Harriman, CIA Director Richard Helms was to warn that the Congolese possessed a 'mercurial temperament' and that the Stanleyville rebels were 'specifically anti-American'. This, Helms believed, was the rebel-held conviction that the US was the driving force behind the counterinsurgency. In his eyes, the advance of the 5th Mechanised Brigade would only add to the 'vulnerability of American hostages.[38]

Ever since 21 August 1964 when Olenga had summarily tried the American diplomats and had sentenced them to death, US

Victims of Simba terror on the streets of Stanleyville.

Hostages massacred by the Simba.

- 20 Boeing KC-135 tanker aircraft of the Strategic Air Command[40]

Though this plan was also shelved due to the time needed to prepare such an operation,[41] within a very short space of time General Adams had put forward another plan codenamed OPLAN 519, or Operation High Beam. This involved using F-4 fighter bombers to destroy enemy installations, an airborne assault by a battalion of paratroopers, and attacking Simba positions. If needed, as second battalion of paratroopers would be dropped over Stanleyville to evacuate the non-Congolese.[42] Separating the head from the body of the rebellion by arresting Soumialot, Olenga and any other rebel leaders, Simba forces would either be forced to surrender or be killed. Though, again, OPLAN 519 was never used, it does bear a striking resemblance to the one eventually used by Colonel Vandewalle at the end of November 1964. Nourished by fresh information provided by an Israeli trader named Narcisse Aldaheff on 2 October, Vandewalle learnt

ambassador McMurtrie Godley had been urging Washington to intervene and rescue the hostages. Though Operation Low Beam had been shelved due to its impracticability, by 15 October the Joint Chiefs of Staff had requested that the Commander in Chief, Strike Command (CINSTRIKE) develop and implement a new rescue plan. Codenamed OPLAN 514 or 'Ready Move 3', devised by General Paul D. Williams, this operation called for the seizing and securing of Stanleyville, the evacuation of non-Congolese, and turning the city over to a friendly government. With a large force needed to overcome a reinforced rebel army, it was thought that a small strike force and an airborne battalion would be required to carry out the initial stages of the operation. A second battalion of US troops would be ready to provide support if needed. The operation would be launched from Wheelus Air Base in Libya just over two days after being given the order, and use Roberts Field Air Base in Liberia, and the Ascension Islands as staging points. US forces under the type of alert needed for this type of operation (DEFCON 4)[39] consisted of:

- Two battalions of soldiers from the 101st Airborne Division
- 16 McDonnell Douglas F-4C Phantom II fighter aircraft
- 60 C-130 transports

that in the panic created by air attacks the Simba had been left to their own devices and were shooting at anything flying over the city. Consequently, Vandewalle believed that the most viable means by which Stanleyville could be liberated was the simultaneous use of airborne and ground troops. Indeed, if both sets were not used in conjunction with one another, it was thought that the lives of a large number of hostages would be in danger and that the hostages would be slaughtered.[43] As Vandewalle correctly deduced, his plan greatly interested authorities in Belgium and in Washington.[44]

While US and Belgian authorities weighed up the possible diplomatic consequences of rescue operations, their commanders and military planners began to examine the finer points of Vandewalle's plan. Among those who were to participate in the planning of operations was Brigadier General Russell E. Dougherty. As the deputy director for plans and operations at the headquarters of US European Command (USEUCOM) in Paris, on 11 November at the US Embassy in Brussels, Dougherty and other officers met several officials from the Belgian Defence Ministry. During these meetings, former commander of the Kamina Air Base Colonel Robert Louvigny described how this military installation opened in 1949 could be used for the launching of a possible attack. Next, accompanied by General Vivario, the Secretary to the Belgian Minister of Defence, Dougherty met with Colonel Charles Laurent,

C-130 Hercules transport planes transported Belgian paratroopers to Stanleyville from Lajes Airfield in the Portuguese Azores on 24 November 1964.

Three C-130s at Kleine Brogel AB.

Belgian paras waiting their turn to embark one of US Hercules transports at Kleine Brogel AB.

deployment of the 1st Parachute Battalion based in Diest in Belgium,[46] and 12 USAF Lockheed C-130s which would fly the 545 Belgian paratroopers from Brussels to Stanleyville via Spain, the Ascension Islands and Kamina military base. The next day, on 16 November Arthur McCafferty of the NSC unveiled the 22-page long OPLAN 319/64, otherwise known as Dragon Rouge, or Red Dragon.[47] As well as containing the details of the Stanleyville operations, these plans also detailed operations in other towns where Belgian lives were in danger. Black Dragon, or Dragon Noir, was the name given to operations in Paulis (Isiro), while White and Green Dragons, or Dragons Blanc and Vert, targeted Bunia and Watsa respectively. All operations would take place on the 24 November 1964 or in the following days.

If the different aspects of the Dragon operations had only been revealed to the NSC on 16 November, by then Colonel Burgess Gradwell of Detachment One of the 322nd Air Division based in Evreux-Fauville had already called up aircrews from the US Tactical Air Command (TAC) who had been assigned to rotational squadrons serving in Europe at the time.[48] Handing each navigator a manila envelope containing flight plans on 17 November, Gradwell and Captain Donald Strobaugh of the 5th Aerial Port Squadron (APRON) took off from France at 1800 hours and headed for Kleine Brogel Air Base situated just outside Brussels. Here, the paratroopers, eight jeeps and 12 motorised tricycles were loaded onto C-130s which promptly left Belgian air space. After a refuelling stop at Morón Air Force Base in southern Spain, the next stage in the journey was the final take-off point situated on the Ascension Islands.[49] Here, the aircraft crews and Belgian troops would await joint permission from both Belgian and US governments to proceed to Stanleyville,[50] and while they were on this British Overseas Territory they would be briefed on the role they were about to play and the logistics of the operations themselves. In a first phase, the planes would travel to Kamina Air Base in Katanga

commander of the Belgian Parachute Regiment. An experienced paratrooper having made several jumps onto Stanleyville airfield during aerial demonstrations in 1959, in the presence of US Ambassador Douglas MacArthur II who had joined the meeting, Laurent laid out his plans for the recapture of Stanleyville airport and how he would employ paratroopers dropped into the landing zones.[45] Just four days after these meetings, William Brubeck of the US National Security Council (NSC) informed presidential advisor McGeorge Bundy that the plan was ready. It involved the

Belgian paratroopers and SAS get underway, 24 November 1964.

and, secondly, forces of the 1st Parachute Battalion would be flown 550 miles north to Stanleyville on five C-130s. Dropping the paratroopers onto a landing zone to the northeast of the city, two other C-130s would then drop the jeeps and other equipment. After 30 minutes, a company of the 2nd Parachute Battalion would fly in as reinforcements.[51]

The Liberation of Stanleyville

With the rescue forces awaiting orders, those given the task of clearing the areas surrounding Stanleyville were making steady progress. After securing control of Kindu in the Maniema province, the next step on the journey north for Mike Hoare was to take the road which led to Mokama, Kabela, and Kipikata and head northwards to Punia some 170 miles away. From here, 5 Commando made its way along the mud-bound tracks that snaked their way through the equatorial forests to Ngeleza and Obokote before arriving in the town of Wanie-Rukula located around 50 miles to the south of Stanleyville. Concurrently, other units of the 5th Mechanised Brigade carried out operations in areas to the north, east and west. These units were 52 Commando which covered on Aketi and Paulis; 53 Commando which covered Beni and Mambasa; and 54 Commando which would attack Ikela and Opala. All were provided air cover by CIA air forces that were used to make strafing runs and destroy enemy transport.[52] Despite setbacks which included the loss of 56 Commando leader Jeremy Spencer,[53] by 20 November and with victory at Punia, the progress made by the combined forces of the 5th Mechanised Brigade brought Vandewalle the hope that both ground and air forces would arrive in Stanleyville at around the same time. Their arrival could not come soon enough for the hundreds of hostages still under siege in the city. Fears for their safety rose as the rebel-controlled radio station announced that '600 Belgian and 60 Americans' had been moved to an unknown destination, and this stoked doubts whether any whites would still be in Stanleyville when the troops arrived.[54]

Although Olenga was clearly not completely of sound mind, he was lucid enough to realise that killing the hostages would take his bargaining chips from the table and would deprive him of the means to negotiate. As the days passed in mid-November, Olenga decided to increase the number of trump cards in his pack by bringing American missionaries into Stanleyville from outlying areas and placing them in detention in the Central Prison or at Camp Ketele. This was the case for Clifford Schaub of Pittsburgh, and Phyllis Rine of Mount Vernon. Kept in confinement, Olenga's limited grasp of reality had deprived them of their spectacles lest they be used to attract enemy aircraft, and much to the amusement of the Simba, they had been forced to dance the cha-cha-cha.[55] On a more serious note, it is important to underline that these hostages remained in grave danger. Beatings were frequent and the threat of execution from a drunken or drugged rebel lay seconds away.

Belgian troops advance through Stanleyville during Operation Red Dragon.

Belgian troops disembark at Simi-Simi Airport, Stanleyville during Operation Red Dragon.

A group of suspected Simbas being forced to lay on the ground while paras are already leading the first group of hostages into a waiting C-130.

Simba positions at Simi-Simi were rapidly overcome and the Simba arrested. Also pictured here are AS.24 motorised tricycles used by Belgian forces.

By the last week of November 1964, the areas around Stanleyville were firmly under the control of Western-backed forces. As Vandewalle waited for the orders allowing these forces to embark on the last stage of their trek through the Congo, last gasp attempts at negotiating the safe release of the hostages were made in order to avoid a potential bloodbath.

On 23 November, for example, US Ambassador to Kenya – William Attwood – met with Kenyan President Jomo Kenyatta, and APL representative Thomas Kanza in Nairobi to discuss a ceasefire. Though these meetings were promising, the position taken by both the Kenyan and rebel army leaders left no doubt as to their outcome: both insisted that the mercenaries leave the Congo forthwith; both denounced what they saw as Tshombe's dependence on the US and Belgium; and both accused the US and Belgium of using the hostage rescue as a pretext for achieving a military objective.[56] Faced with the refusal to cooperate, and with Tshombe and Mobutu already having approved the rescue operations, Red Dragon was launched on 24 November.[57]

At his base in Kindu, at 0230 hours that Tuesday morning, the Makasi's Reginaldo Blanco was handed a weather report, navigational charts and aerial photos of Stanleyville taken the day before from a specially-equipped Boeing C-97 Stratofreighter. Joined in the cockpit of his B-26 by Belgian Colonel Avi Bouzin, Blanco then received flight plans instructing him to head north-west to Isangi, then south-east to Stanleyville. Bouzin was an important passenger due to the fact that he had been given the mission of coordinating the parachute drop, the attack by the two Lima columns, and the attacks to be made by Cuban-piloted bombers and fighter

Europeans were massacred in other areas controlled by the Simba.

Belgian paras mounted on one of their semi-armoured Land Rover Minervas shortly after landing at Paulis airport during Operation Dragon Noir.

planes. Arriving at Isangi just as the sun appeared over the horizon, the plan also included leaving two minutes ahead of the C-130s in order to make strafing runs over Simi-Simi airfield. At 0545,[58] Blanco, and Makasi pilots Castor Cereceda Coira, Thomas Afont, and Francisco Alvarez then attacked Simba defences.[59] With the successful elimination of ground artillery, the path was now clear for the arrival of the USAF C-130s.

Departing at 0245[60] that same morning, Chalks 1 to 5 firstly flew to Basoko some 120 miles northwest of Stanleyville where they were to rendezvous with other elements of the Makasi. Green-lighted by the dispatchers aboard Chalk 1, Captain Warren 'Huey' Long offloaded his cargo of paratroopers from Company 11 led by Colonel Laurent onto the airfield and golf course which lay on the airfield's perimeter. Though Long and the other C-130s received groundfire from Soviet DShK M38 heavy machine guns and Browning machine guns captured from the ANC, the Simba only managed to inflict slight damage.[61] In all, it took around 80 seconds for the initial 320 paratroopers to disembark. With the airfield secured after attacking the control tower and disabling Simba weapons, the next step was to clear the runaway so that Chalks 7 to 9 could land. The Simba had made this problematical as they had littered the runway with vehicles and other detritus. Having received intelligence that hostages were being held at the Hotel Victoria on the corner of Avenue Maurice Lippens and Avenue Sergent Ketele, Company 11 was ordered to advance along Avenue Monseigneur Grison and the Avenue de Gaulle. If they made rapid progress into the centre of Stanleyville, however, when the red berets arrived on the Avenue de l'Eglise they were greeted by a petrified Belgian who informed them that they were too late and that murder was already being committed.[62]

The suspicions of those confined to the Hotel Victoria that some sort of mission was under way were raised when the noise of the rescue aircraft appeared in the skies above Stanleyville. All flights having been stopped for some time,

Paras guiding a group of nuns towards the airport.

A captured Simba is led past another Land Rover Minerva at Paulis with a US C-130 transport in the background.

what had once been a familiar sound was now unusual. Inside the hotel Donald Parkes, James Stauffer, and Ernie Houle wondered how their Simba guards would react.[63] The answer was not long in coming as at 7 a.m. the Americans and 250 other hostages were ordered to leave their rooms and to descend onto the street below.[64] Fearing the worst, other hostages managed to escape and hid on the roof of the building or in cupboards and wardrobes. Those who now stood in front of the hotel were greeted by rebel leader Colonel Opepe. Visibly angry and accompanied by Simba carrying automatic weapons which they held to the heads of child hostages, Opepe ordered the Americans and Belgians to form ranks of three and to march to the airport. They were to be used as human shields against any further landings.[65] Among them were Nothomb, Hoyt, Grinwiss, Rine, Carlson and Belgian national Michelle Peneff. She, her husband Marco, and her children had spent months at the hotel.[66]

As the column reached the junction of Avenue Sergeant Ketele and Avenue Lothaire, the loud bursts of automatic gunfire coming from the Belgian paratroopers making their way along Avenue Monseigneur Grison alerted Opepe who ordered his men to open fire on the hostages. Shouting "Ciyuga! Ciyuga!" or "kill them", the Simba began to systematically massacre anyone with white skin. Some of the hostages, like one six-year-old girl, died immediately. Mown in half by Simba bullets,[67] she joined Marco Peneff who was shot in the head at close range, and despite his wife's efforts to save him by blocking his wound with her finger, Peneff died then and there on the pavement. Michelle Peneff had also been hit in the chest and a bullet had lodged itself in her lung.[68] In total, 22 hostages including Dr. Carlson and Phyllis Rine were either shot or hacked to death by the Simba on 24 November.

There were a number of survivors of the Stanleyville massacre including the son of prominent Nazi, Martin Bormann,[69] and Charles E. Davis, his wife and two children, Stephen aged four, and Beth aged 20 months. Some months later, Beth would feature on the cover of *Paris Match* where she was pictured in the arms of one of her rescuers.[70]

9
Epilogue

To all intents and purposes Guevara's attempt to subvert the authority of the Congolese state was the last serious threat to the country's integrity. Though the so-called 'Mercenary Revolt' in 1967 briefly renewed the threat of insurgency, Mobutu's second coup d'Etat which took place just five days after Guevara's departure from the Congo sealed his place as the one-man president and set him on the road to becoming one of Africa's strong men. Supported militarily and financially by the United States, but making overtures to Katangan forces and Simba rebels by encouraging them to join the ANC in 1966, Mobutu also showed that he was prepared to bring the Congo back into the fold of mainstream African politics by organising and chairing a conference of the OAU held in Kinshasa in September 1967.

As for Mobutu's potential rivals and former foes, little by little they were either eliminated, tortured to death, or placated with offers of peace and power: Evariste Kimba, prime minister for just over a month in October and November 1965 was hanged for treason; three other former ministers – Jérôme Anany, Emmanuel Bamba and Alexandre Mahamba – were hanged with him; and, as we saw earlier, Pierre Mulele and fellow insurgent Théophile Bengila were brutally slaughtered. Whereas Moïse Tshombe was dismissed by Kasa-Vubu and, again, sought the safety of exile in Spain in October 1965, he too would meet an untimely death in an Algerian jail in 1969. His name becoming synonymous with the 'selling out' of the Congo's wealth to Western interests,[1] Antoine Gizenga preferred to seek out more comfortable political surroundings by leaving for Congo-Brazzaville in November 1965. He then travelled to Moscow, Egypt, Guinea, Mali and Ghana in 1973 to solicit support against Mobutu and to voice support for Laurent-Désiré Kabila's

Evacuation of wounded hostages to a waiting Hercules.

A look into the cargo hold of a C-130, full of stretchers with wounded evacuees.

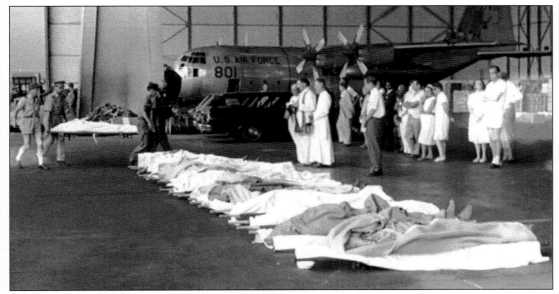
The bodies of some of the hostages killed by the Simba await repatriation.

pro-Chinese movement in the then eastern Zaire.[2] As for this leading member of the CNL, he became a dyed in the wool Marxist. Setting up the People's Revolutionary Party (PRP) in South Kivu in 1967, Kabila would play a leading role in the First Congo War which began in October 1996. Unlike Gizenga and Mulele before him, Kabila succeeded in overthrowing a sitting government in 1997 but, like Lumumba, Tshombe and Mulele, died an unnatural death when he was shot and killed in January 2001 aged 61. CNL leader Christophe Gbenye fled to Uganda in 1966 and died in Kinshasa in 2010 aged 83. Other than his dying in November 2006, not much is known about Gaston Soumialot. Nicholas Olenga was reportedly killed in Congo-Brazzaville in 1986. The last of the so-called Lumumbists, Gizengists, and Mulelists, Thomas Kanza went on to have a successful career as a writer, academic, politician and diplomat. Dying from a heart attack in London in 2004 while serving as the Congo's ambassador to Sweden, Kanza had formerly been a minister in Kabila's revolutionary government.

Bibliography

United States Government Archival Documents

'Briefing Paper Prepared in the Department of State', Washington, undated, FRUS 1961-1963, Document 7.

Foreign Relations of the United States, Vol. XXIII, *Congo, 1960-1968* (Washington: United States Government Printing Office, 2013).

'National Security Council Meeting' Washington, 25 July 1960, Central Intelligence Agency Files, Job 79R00890A, Box 13, Folder, NSC Briefings, July 1960.

CIA Cable, 'Leopoldville to Director', 15 August 1960, FRUS, Vol. XXIII, Congo, D419.

CIA Cable, 'Leopoldville to Director', 18 August 1960, FRUS, Vol. XXIII, Congo, D421.

CIA Cable, 'Leopoldville to Director', 24 August 1960, FRUS, Vol. XXIII, Congo, D427.

'Telegram from the Embassy in the Congo to the Department of State', August 29 1960, FRUS, Vol. XXIII, D192.

'US Consulate in Elisabethville Cable No.576 to US State Department', 3 January 1961.

'Special National Intelligence Estimate 65-61', 10 January 1961, FRUS, Vol.XXI, Africa, D2.

'Telegram from the Embassy in the Congo to the Department of State', 10 January 1961, FRUS, Vol. XXI, Africa, D3.

'Memorandum of Conversation', Washington, 26 January 1961, FRUS, Vol.XXI, Africa, D11.

'US Embassy in Leopoldville Cable No.1835 to US State Department', 3 February 1961.

'Memorandum from Williams to Rusk', 7 February 1961, Dept. of State, NSC Files, Lot 70, D265.

'The Volta River and Related Projects', Washington, 17 February 1961, FRUS, Vol.XXI, Africa, D223.

'Memorandum of Conversation', Washington', 8 March 1961, FRUS, Vol.XXI, Africa, D225.

'US Embassy in Leopoldville Cable No.1847 to US State Department', 3 April 1961.

'Telegram from the Department of State to the Embassy in the Congo', Washington, 26 May 1964, FRUS, Vol. XXIII, Congo, D172.

'Memorandum for President Johnson', Washington, 15 June 1964, FRUS, Vol. XXIII, Congo, D177.

'Memorandum from the Director of the United States Information Agency (Rowan) to President Johnson, Washington, 19 June 1964, FRUS, Vol. XXIII, Congo, D20.

'Telegram from the Department of State to the Embassy in Spain', Washington, 22 June 1964, FRUS, Vol. XXIII, Congo, D181

'Memorandum from the Joint Strategic Survey Council to the Joint Chiefs of Staff', Washington, 25 June 1964, FRUS, Vol. XXIII, Congo, D182.

'Memorandum From the Under Secretary of State for Political Affairs (Harriman) to the President's Special Assistant for National Security Affairs (Bundy)', Washington, 11 July 1964, FRUS, Vol. XXIII, Congo, D189.

'Telegram From the Department of State to the Embassy in Belgium', Washington, 6 August 1964, FRUS, Vol. XXIII, Congo, D197.

'Memorandum from the Deputy Director of the Office of Central African Affairs (Looram) to the Assistant Secretary of State for African Affairs (Williams)', Washington, 19 September 1964, FRUS, Vol. XXIII, Congo, D260.

'Telegram from the Department of State to the Embassy in Kenya', Washington 22 September 1964, FRUS, Vol. XXIII, Congo, D261.

'Memorandum from the Deputy Director for Plans, Central Intelligence Agency (Helms) to the Under Secretary of State for Political Affairs (Harriman)', 14 October 1964, FRUS, Vol. XXIII, Congo, D284.

'Memorandum from Arthur McCafferty of the National Security Council Staff to the President's Special Assistant for National Security Affairs (Bundy)', *Planning for evacuation of US personnel from Stanleyville*, 15 October 1964, FRUS, Vol. XXIII, Congo, D285.

'Telegram from the Department of State to the Embassy in Belgium', Washington, 28 October 1964, FRUS, Vol. XXIII, Congo, D304.

'Telegram from the Department of State to the Embassy in Belgium', 16 November 1964, FRUS, Vol. XXIII, Congo, D325.

'Telegram from the Embassy in the Congo to the Department of State', 21 November 1964, FRUS, Vol. XXIII, Congo, D345.

'Telegram from the Embassy in Kenya to the Department of State', 23 November 1964, FRUS, Vol. XXIII, Congo, D350.

'Circular Telegram from the Department of State to Certain African Posts', 27 November 1964, FRUS, Vol. XXIII, Congo, D364.

'Memorandum from the Director of the United States Information Agency (Rowan) to President Johnson, Washington, 19 June 1964, FRUS, Vol. XXIII, Congo, D20.

'Telegram from the Department of State to the Embassy in Belgium', Washington, 28 October 1964, FRUS, Vol. XXIII, Congo, D304.

'Memorandum from Robert W. Kromer of the National Security Council to the President's Special Assistant for National Security Affairs (Bundy)', 26 January 1965, Johnson Library, National Security File, Country File, Congo, Vol. X.

'Memorandum for the Record', 26 January 1965, FRUS, Vol. XXIII, Congo, D392.

'Memorandum from Robert W. Komer of the National Security Council Staff to the President's Special Assistant for Security Affairs, Washington, 26 March 1965', Johnson Library, National Security File, Country File, Congo, Vol. XI, Memos & Miscellaneous, 1/65-9/65, Secret.

'Memorandum from the Chief of the Africa Division, Directorate of Plans, Central Intelligence Agency (Fields) to Assistant Secretary of State for African Affairs (Williams)', 28 April 1965, Central Intelligence Agency Files, Job 76-00366R, DDO/ISO Files, Box 1, Folder 8, Congo, 1960-1969, Part II, Secret.

'Memorandum from Harold H. Saunders of the National Security Council Staff to President Johnson', 25 February 1965, Johnson Library, National Security File, Congo, Vol. XI, Memos & Miscellaneous, 1/65-9/65, Secret.

'Memorandum from the President's Special Assistant for National Security Affairs (Bundy) to President Johnson, 25 August 1965', Johnson Library, National Security File, Country File, Congo, Vol. XI, Memos & Miscellaneous, 1/65-9/65, Secret.

'Memorandum for the 303 Committee, 24 September 1965', National Security Council, Intelligence Files, Congo 1960-1965, Secret: Eyes Only.

'Memorandum for President Johnson, 29 September 1965', National Security Council, Intelligence Files, Congo 1960-1965, Secret; Eyes Only.

'Alleged Assassination Plots Involving Foreign Leaders', US Senate Select Committee to Study Governmental Operations (Washington D.C.: US Government Printing Office, 1975).

Congolese Government Archival Documents

'Republic of the Congo (Léopoldville), The Province of the Katanga and Congolese Independence', *Document Division of the Ministry of Foreign Affairs*, Number 1, January, 1962.

'Livre blanc du Gouvernement katangais sur les activités des hors-la-loi dans certains territoires baluba' (Elisabethville: Gouvernement katangais, 1961).

UN Documents

'Report of the Security Council Commission of Inquiry Established under Resolution 496 (1981)', Security Council Official Records, United Nations, 1982.

'UN Security Council Resolution 161' [The Congo Question] UN Security Council, 21 February 1961.

'Questions Concerning the Situation in the Republic of the Congo (Leopoldville)', Chapter VII, pp.60-61, https://www.un.org/Depts/dhl/dag/docs/congo61.pdf, accessed 21 May 2019.

Speeches and Personal Correspondence (by date)

Patrice Lumumba, 'Speech at Accra, 1958', available at https://www.blackpast.org/global-african-history/1958-patrice-lumumba-speech-accra/, accessed 14 May 2019.

Patrice Lumumba, 'Speech given at the Congress for the Freedom of Culture', Ibadan, Nigeria, March 22 1959, available at https://www.marxists.org/subject/africa/lumumba/1960/08/25.htm, accessed 20 June 2019.

'From a letter to Dag Hammarskjöld, U.N. Secretary-General, August 14 1960', available at https://www.marxists.org/subject/africa/lumumba/1960/08/umgensec.htm, accessed 27 June 2019.

'Speech of Dr. Fidel Castro at the UN General Assembly, September 1960', available at http://www1.lanic.utexas.edu/project/castro/db/1960/19600926.html, accessed 23 June 2018.

'Ernesto Guevara speech in Santiago de Cuba, 30 November, 1964', available at http://www.politique-actu.com/dossier/ernesto-guevara-discours-historique-anniversaire/1702290/, accessed 3 June 2019.

'Ernesto Guevara's speech at the Afro-Asian Conference in Algeria', 24 February 1965, The Che Reader, Ocean Press, 2005, reproduced by https://www.marxists.org/archive/guevara/1965/02/24.htm, accessed 3 June, 2019.

'Farewell letter from Che to Fidel Castro' 1 April 1965, available at https://www.marxists.org/archive/guevara/1965/04/01.htm, accessed 23 June 2019.

Published Sources

Abbot, Peter, *Armies in East Africa* (Oxford: Osprey Publishing, 2002).

Akeampong, Emmanuel Kwaku, and Gates, Henry Louis, *Dictionary of African Biography* (New York: OUP, 2012).

Anderson, John Lee, *Che Guevara: A Revolutionary Life* (London: Bantam Press, 1997).

Attwood, William, *The Reds and the Blacks: A Personal Adventure* (New York: Harper and Row, 1967).

Bamford, James, *Body of Secrets: Anatomy of the Ultra-Secret National Security Agency* (First Anchor Books, 2002).

Banjikila, Thomas *Epuration ethnique en Afrique*: les 'Kasaians', Katanga 1961-Shaba 1992 (Paris: L'Harmattan, 1997).

Bethune, Arm., *Le Katanga, Province Belge* (Paris: Broché, 2010).

Brausch, Georges, *Belgian Administration in the Congo* (Oxford: OUP, 1961).

Brion, R., and Moreau, J-L., *De la mine à Mars: La Genèse d'Umicore* (Brussels: Lannoo, 2006).

Bula-Bula, Théophile, *Pierre Mulele et le maquis du Kwilu en R.D. Congo* (Paris: L'Harmattan, 2010).

Buttgenbach, M.H., *Les mines du Katanga* (Brussels: Imprimerie A. Lesigne, 1908).

Collier, Paul, and Sambanis, Nicholas (eds.) *Understanding Civil War (Volume 1: Africa) Evidence and Analysis* (World Bank: 2005).

Cornet, René, *La bataille du rail* (Brussels: Editions L. Cuypers, 1953).

Crawford, Daniel, *Thinking Black: 22 Years without a Break in the Long Grass* (George H. Doran: New York, 1912).

Cruise O'Brien, Connor, *To Katanga and Back* (London: Four Square Books, 1965).

De Vos, Luc, Gérard, Emmanuel, Gérard-Libois, Jules, and Raxhorn, Philippe, *Les secrets de l'affaire Lumumba* (Bruxelles: Editions Racine, 2005).

Devlin, Larry, *Chief of Station, Congo* (New York: Public Affairs, 2008).

Dreke, Victor, *From Escambray to the Congo: In the Whirlwind of the Cuban Revolution* (Pathfinder Press, 2002).

Duchemin, Jaques, Le Bailly, Jaques, and Trinquier, Roger, *Notre guerre au Katanga* (Paris: Editions de la pensée moderne, 1963).

Dumbrell, John, *President Johnson and Soviet Communism* (Manchester: Manchester University Press, 2012).

Edgerton, Robert B., *The Troubled Heart of Africa: A History of the Congo* (St. Martin's Press: New York, 2002).

Fox Bourne, Henry Richard, *Civilisation in Congoland, a Story of International Wrong-Doing* (London: P.S King & Son, 1903).

George, Edward, *The Cuban Intervention in Angola, 1965-1991: From Che Guevara to Cuito Cuanavale* (New York & London: Frank Cass, 2005).

Gérard-Libois, Jules and Verhaegen, Benoit, *Congo 1960, Tome 2* (Brussels: CRISP, 1963).

Gérard-Libois, Jules and Verhaegen, Benoit, *Congo 1965: Political Documents of a Developing Nation* (New Jersey: Princeton University Press, 2015).

Gérard-Libois, Jules, and Verhaegen, Benoit, *Congo 1960* (Brussels: Dossiers du CRISP, 1961).

Gérard-Libois, Jules, *Secession au Katanga* (Brussels: CRISP 1963).

Gleijeses, Piero, *Conflicting Missions: Havana, Washington, and Africa, 1959-1976* (North Carolina: North Carolina University Press, 2003).

Guevara, Ernesto, *Guerilla Warfare: A Method* (Peking: Foreign Language Press, 1964).

Guevara, Ernesto, *The African Dream: The Diaries of the Revolutionary War in the Congo* (London: The Harvill Press, 2000).

Hamilton, Lowell, *Men, Wars and Sex of the 60's* (Bloomington: Author House, 2017).

Haskin, Jeanne M., *The Tragic State of the Congo: from Decolonization to Dictatorship* (New York: Algora Publishing, 2005).

Hawes, James, and Koenig, Mary Ann, *Cold War Navy Seal: Che Guevara, CIA Black Ops, and My Experience as the First Seal in Africa* (New York: Skyhorse Publishing, 2018).

Hoare, Mike, *Congo Mercenary* (Boulder, CO: Paladin, 2008).

Hoare, Mike, *The Road to Kalamata: A Congo Mercenary's Personal Memoir* (Boulder, CO: Paladin Press, 1989).

Horne, Gerald, *Mau Mau in Harlem?: The US and the Liberation of Kenya* (New York: Palgrave Macmillan, 2009).

Hoskyns, Catherine, *The Congo since Independence: January 1960-December 1961* (New York: Oxford University Press, 1965).

Jowett, Philip, *Modern African Wars: The Nigerian-Biafran War* (London: Osprey Publishing, 2016).

Kabuya Lumuna Sando, Célestin, *Nord-Katanga 1960-1964. De la Sécession à la guerre civile. Le meurtre des chefs* (Paris: L'Harmattan, 1992).

Kalb, Madeleine, *The Congo Cables: The Cold War in Africa-From Eisenhower to Kennedy* (London: Macmillan, 1982).

Kalonji Mulopwe, Albert, *Dossier du massacre des Baluba à Bakwanga de 1960* (Kinshasa: Conférence nationale souveraine, 1992).

Kashamura, Anicet, *De Lumumba aux colonels* (Paris: Broché, 1966).

Kelly, Sean, *America's Tyrant: the CIA and Mobutu of Zaire* (Washington DC: American University Press, 1993).

Kennes, Erik, and Larmer, Miles, *The Katangese Gendarmes and War in Central Africa: Fighting their Way Home* (Bloomington: Indiana University Press, 2016).

Kryza, Frank T., *The Race for Timbuktu: In Search of Africa's City of Gold* (New York: Harper Collins, 2006).

La Fontaine, J.S., *City Politics: A Study of Léopoldville*, (Cambridge: At the University Press, 1970).

Labrique, Jean, *Congo politique* (Leopoldville: Editions de l'Avenir, 1957).

Lantier, Jaques, *Le temps des mercenaires* (Paris: CAL, 1969).

Legum, Colin, *Congo Disaster* (Baltimore: Penguin Books, 1960).

Livingstone, David, *The Last Journals of David Livingstone in Central Africa* (New York: Harper and Brothers Limited, 1875).

Martens, Ludo, *Pierre Mulele, ou, La seconde vie de Lumumba* (Brussels: EPO, 1985).

McGowan, Sam, *Anything, Anywhere, Anytime* (Bloomington: AuthorHouse, 2011).

Meriwether, James Hunter, *Proudly We Can be Africans, Black Americans and Africa, 1935-1961* (North Carolina: University of North Carolina Press, 2002).

Meriwether, James Hunter, *The African Connection and the Struggle for Freedom: Africa's Role in American Life* (Los Angeles: University of California, 1995).

Mockler, Anthony, *Mercenaries* (London: Macdonald, 1969).

Mwakikagile, Godfrey, *Africa, 1960-1970: Chronicle and Analysis* (Dar Es Salaam: New Africa Press, 2014).

Nzongola-Ntalaja, Georges, *From Leopold to Kabila: A People's History* (London: Zed Books, 2002).

Oliver, Roland, and Atmore, Anthony, *Medieval Africa, 1250-1800* (Cambridge: Cambridge University Press, 2001).

Othen, Christopher, *Katanga 1960-63: Mercenaries, Spies and the African Nation that Waged War on the World* (The History Press, 2015).

Packham, Eric S., *Freedom and Anarchy* (Nova Science Publishers, Inc., 1996).

Pasteger, Romain, *Le Visage des affreuxmercenaires Katangais* (Paris: Broché, 2004).

Puren, Jeremy, and Pottinger, Brian, *Mecenary Commander* (South Africa: Galago Publishing, 1986).

Reed, David, *111 Days in Stanleyville* (London: Collins, 1966).

Samarin, William J., *The Black Man's Burden: African Colonial Labor on the Congo and Ubangi Rivers, 1880-1900* (Boulder: Westview Press, 1989).

Sasser, Charles W., and Hamilton, William H., *Night Fighter: an Insider's Story of Special Ops from Korea to Seal Team 6* (New York: Arcade Publishing, 2016).

Scholl-Latour, Peter, *Mort sur le grand fleuve. Du Congo au Zaïre, chronique d'une indépendance* (Paris: Presses de la Cité, 1988).

Sibanda, Eliakim, *The Zimbabwe African People's Union 1961-1987: A Political History of Insurgency in Southern Rhodesia* (Africa World Press, 2005).

Soret, Marcel, *Les Kongo Nord-Occidentaux* (Paris: L'Harmattan, 1959), 21, in Verhaegen, *L'ABAKO et l'indépendance du Congo belge: dix ans de nationalisme kongo* (Paris: L'Harmattan, 2003).

Trento, Joseph J., *Prelude to Terror: Edwin P. Wilson and the Legacy of America's Private Intelligence Network* (New York: Carrol & Graf Publishers, 2005).

Trinquier, Roger, *Modern Warfare: A French View of Counterinsurgency* (London and Dunmow: Pall Mall Press, 1964).

Van Bilsen, A. A. J., *Vers l'indépendance du Congo et du Ruanda-Urundi* (Kinshasa: Presses Universitaires, 1977).

Vanderstraeten, Louis-François, *La répression de la révolte des Pende du Kwango en 1931* (Brussels: Académie Royale des Sciences d'Outre-mer, 2001).

Vandewalle, E.R., *L'Ommegang: Odyssée & Reconquête de Stanleyville, 1964* (Brussels: Le Livre Africain, 1970).

Vanthemsche, Guy, *Belgium and the Congo* (Cambridge: Cambridge University Press, 2011).

Vellut, Jean-Luc, 'Mining in the Belgian Congo', in David Birmingham and Phyllis M. Martin (eds), *History of Central Africa* (New York and London: Longman, 1983).

Verhaegen, Benoit *Rebellions au Congo* (Brussels: CRISP, 1966).

Verhaegen, Benoit, *ABAKO, 1950-1960* (Brussels: Dossiers du CRISP, 1963).

Verhaegen, Benoit, *Congo 1961* (Brussels: CRISP, 1962).

Verhaegen, Benoit, *L'ABAKO et l'indépendance du Congo belge: dix ans de nationalisme kongo* (Paris: L'Harmattan, 2003).

Verhaegen, Benoit, *Mulele et la révolution populaire au Kwilu* (Paris: L'Harmattan, 2006).

Villafaña, Frank, *Cold War in the Congo: The Confrontation of Cuban Military Forces, 1960-1967* (New Brunswick: Transaction Publishers, 2009).

Vlassenroot, Koen, *South Kivu: Identity, territory, and power in the eastern Congo* (London: Rift Valley Institute, 2013).

Wagoner, Fred E., *Dragon Rouge: The Rescue of the Hostages* (University Press of the Pacific, 2003).

Warnock, Timothy (ed.), *Short of War: Major USAF Contingency Operations* (Air Force History and Museums Program, 2000).

Weigert, Stephen L., *Traditional Religion and Guerrilla Warfare in Modern Africa* (New York: St. Martin's Press, 1996).

Weiner, Tim, *Legacy of the Ashes: The History of the CIA* (London: Penguin Books, 2007).

Weiss, Herbert, F., *Political Protest in the Congo: the Parti Solidaire Africain during the Independence Struggle* (Princeton NJ: Princeton University Press, 1967).

Welch, Claude Emerson, *Anatomy of Rebellion* (SUNY Press, 1980).

Willame, Jean-Claude, *Patrimonialism and Political Change in the Congo* (Stanford: Stanford University Press, 1972).

Witte, Ludo de, *The Assassination of Lumumba* (Brussels: Karthala, 2000).

Young, Crawford, *Politics in the Congo: Decolonization and Independence* (Oxford: OUP, 1965).

Young, Crawford, *Politics in the Congo: Decolonization and Independence* (New Jersey: Princeton University Press, 2015).

Zeilig, Leo, *Lumumba: Africa's Lost Leader* (London: Haus, 2008).

Zeilig, Leo, Renton, David, and Seddon, David, *The Congo: Plunder and Resistance* (London: Zed Books, 2007).

Articles published in journals

Clarke, J.J.G., 'The Congo Mercenary: A History and Analysis', *The South African Institute of International Affairs*, Johannesburg, 1968.

Comhaire, J., 'Some Aspects of Urbanization in the Belgian Congo', *American Journal of Sociology*, No.42, July 1956.

Covington-Ward, Yolanda, 'Joseph Kasa-Vubu, ABAKO? and Performances of Kongo Nationalism in the Independence of Congo', *Journal of Black Studies*, Special issue: 1960s Africa in Historical Perspective, Vol.43, No.1, January 2012.

Crowley, Daniel J., 'Politics and Tribalism in the Katanga', *The Western Political Quarterly*, Vol.16, No.1, March 1963.

'Excerpts from Prof. Van Bilsen's 'Thirty Year Plan', in 'Conflict in the Congo', *Africa Today*, Vol.7, No.5, September 1960.

Fetter, Bruce S., 'The Luluabourg Revolt at Elisabethville', *African Historical Studies*, Vol. 2, No. 2, 1969.

Flintham, Victor, *Air Wars and Aircraft: A Detailed Record of Air Combat, 1945 to the Present* (New York: Facts on File, 1990).

Fox, Renee C., de Craemer, Willy, and Ribeaucourt, Jean-Marie, 'The Second Independence': A Case Study of the Kwilu Rebellion in the Congo', *Comparative Studies in Society and History*, Vol.8, No.1, October 1965.

Dodenhoff, George H., 'The Congo: A Case Study of Mercenary Employment', *Naval College Review*, April 1969.

Gleijeses, Piero, 'Cuba's First Venture in Africa: Algeria, 1961-1965', *Journal of Latin American Studies*, 1996.

Gonze, Colin, 'Katanga Secession: The New Colonialism', *Africa Today*, Vol.9, No.1, February 1962.

Hance, William A., and Van Dongen, Irene S., 'The Port of Lobito and the Benguela Railway', *Geographical Review*, Vol.46, No.4, October 1956.

Harms, Robert, 'The End of Red Rubber: A Reassessment', *The Journal of African History*, Volume 16, Issue 1, January 1975.

Hiernaux, J., 'Luba du katanga et Luba du Kasai (Congo): comparaison de deux populations de même origine', *Bulletins et Mémoires de la Société d'Anthropologie de Paris*, 1964.

Heywood, Linda, 'Slavery and its Transformation in the Kingdom of the Kongo: 1491-1800', *The Journal of African History*, Vol.50, No.1, 2009.

Houser, George M., 'A Report on the All African People's Conference Held in Accra, Ghana, December 8-13, 1958', *American Committee on Africa*, New York, 1959.

Jewsiewicki, Bogumil, Lema, Kilola, and Vellut, Jean-Luc, 'Documents pour servir de l'histoire sociale du Zaire: grèves dans le Bas-Congo en 1945', *Etudes d'histoire africaine*, 1973.

Kabuya Lumuna Sando, Célestin, 'Laurent Désiré Kabila', *Review of African Political Economy*, Vol.29, No.93/94, September 2002.

Larmer, Miles, 'Of Local Identities and Transnational Conflict: the Katangese Gendarmes and Central-Southern Africa's Forty-year war, 1960-1999', in Nir Arielli and Bruce Collins (eds.), *Transnational Soldiers: Foreign Military Enlistment in the Modern Era* (London: Palgrave Macmillan, 2013).

Laumann, Dennis, Che Guevara's Visit to Ghana, *Transactions of the Historical Society of Ghana*, New Series, No. 9, 2005.

Lavry, Jaques, and Raymaekers, Paul,'Conjonctures socio-économiques à Léopoldville', 5e Bulletin, Situation au 15 Décembre 1961, *Notes et Documents*, Vol. II, n° 2/SE-2, (Léopoldville: Université Lovanium, Institut de Recherches Economiques et Sociales), décembre 1961.

Legum, Colin, 'The Belgian Congo: Revolt of the Elite', *Africa South*, Vol.4, No.1, October-December 1959.

Rene Lemarchand, 'The Limits of Self-Determination: The Case of the Katanga Secession', *The American Political Science Review*, Vol.56, No.2, June 1962.

Lemarchand, Rene, 'The Bases of Nationalism among the Bakongo', *Africa: Journal of the International African Institute*, Vol.31, No.4, October 1961.

Lemarchand, René, 'The Democratic Republic of Congo: From Collapse to Potential Reconstruction', Occasional Paper, *Centre of African Studies*, University of Copenhagen, September 2001,

Massie, Michael, 'An Analysis of Mao Tse-Tung's Three Main Rules of Discipline and Eight Points for Attention', *American Historical Association Faculty Development Program*, Stony Brook University, 1977.

Mazov, Sergei, 'Soviet Aid to the Gizenga Government in the Former Belgian Congo (1960-61) as Reflected in Russian Archives', *Cold War History*, Vol. 7, No. 3, August 2007.

Nicolaï, Henri, 'Naissance d'une région en Afrique centrale: Le Kwilu', *Les Cahiers d'Outre-Mer*, 1964.

Odom, Thomas P., 'Dragon Operations: Hostage Rescues in the Congo, 1964-1965', Leavenworth Papers, Number 14, *Combat Studies Institute*, Fort Leavenworth, Kansas, 1986.

Rubbens, A., 'Political Awakening in the Congo', *Civilisations*, Vol.10, No.1, 1960.

Shaftel, David, 'The Black Eagle of Harlem', *Air & Space Magazine*, December 2008.

Slade, Ruth M., 'King Leopold's Congo: Aspects of the Development of Race Relations in the Congo Independent State', *Institute of Race Relations* (Oxford, OUP, 1962).

Stanard, Mathew, 'Bilan du monde pour un monde plus déshumanisé': The 1958 Brussels World Fair and Belgian Perceptions of the Congo', *European History Quarterly*, 1 April 2005, Vol.35, Issue 2, pp.267-298.

Weaver Jr, Harold D., 'Paul Robeson and the Pan-African World', *Présence Africaine*, No.107, 3 trimester, 1978.

Yakemtchouk, Romain, 'Aux origines du séparatisme katangais', Académie Royale des Sciences d'Outre-Mer, Classe des Sciences Morales et Politiques, *Mémoires in-8*, Nouvelle Série, Tome 50, Fasc. 1, Brussels, 1988.

Young, Crawford, 'Background to Independence', *Transition*, No.25, 1966.

Young, Crawford, 'Rebellion and the Congo', in Robert I. Rotberg (ed.) *Rebellion in Black Africa* (London: OUP, 1971).

'Les problèmes au Katanga', *Courrier hebdomadaire du CRISP*, Vol.55, No.9, 1960.

Official Reports and Biographies (by date)

'A Manual of Belgian Congo', *Geographical Section of the Naval Intelligence Division*, Naval Staff, Admiralty, (London: His Majesty's Stationery Office, 1891).

Boone, Olga, *Carte ethnique du Congo: quart sud-est* (Tervuern, Royal Museum for Central Africa, 1961).

Lloyd Winterbottom, Harold St. John,et al., *The Belgian Congo* (Great Britain: Naval Intelligence Division, 1944).

'Louis Marie François Frank', Biographie Coloniale Belge, *Institut Royale de la colonie belge*, Tome III, 1952.

'Les problèmes du travail en Afrique', *International Labour Office*, Geneva, 1959.

'Rapport sur les salaires dans la République du Congo', *International Labour Office*, Geneva, 1960.

'Tshombe, Moïse-Kapenda', *Biographie Belge d'Outre-Mer* (Brussels: Académie Royale des Sciences d'Outre-mer, Tome VII-A).

William Edward Burghardt Du Bois, 'Fifth Pan-African Congress final resolution', October 1945, W. E. B. Du Bois Papers (MS

312). Special Collections and University Archives, University of Massachusetts Amherst Libraries.

Various Documents from Digital Sources

'2nd Summit Conference of Heads of State or Government of the Non-Aligned Movement, Cairo, Egypt, October 1964', available at http://cns.miis.edu/nam/documents/Official_Document/2nd_Summit_FD_Cairo_Declaration_1964.pdf, accessed 24 June 2018.

Department of Defense Dictionary of Military and Associated Terms, 12 April 2001, https://web.archive.org/web/20091108082044/http://www.dtic.mil/doctrine/jel/new_pubs/jp1_02.pdf, accessed 4 August 2017.

Haulman, Daniel L., 'Congolese Mercy Airlift', *Air Mobility Command Museum*, (date unknown) available at https://amcmuseum.org/history/congolese-mercy-airlift/, accessed 1 July 2019.

'Les Géants du Cuivre: Leçons tirées des Entreprises Etatiques Minières en RDC et en Zambie', *Natural Resource Governance Institute*, undated, available at https://www.resourcegovernance.org/sites/default/files/documents/nrgi_nmc_french.pdf, accessed April 2017.

'Loi fondamentale sur la structure de l'Etat du Congo belge', May 1960, available at, https://leganet.cd/Legislation/Droit%20Public/Loi%20fondamentale%201960.pdf, accessed 24 May 2019.

'Loi du 14 août 1962 sur la création des provinces de Kwango, Kwilu et Mai-Ndombe', available at www.droitcongolais.info, accessed 20 April 2019.

'Lumumba-Mulele-Kabila', *Révolution Congolaise*, No.1, 3 October 2003, 4, available at www.deboutcongolais.info, accessed 5 June 2019.

'Patrice Lumumba, First Prime Minister of the Congo, June 30, 1960', https://africanlegends.files.wordpress.com/2011/06/patrice-lumumba-speech.pdf, accessed 6 September 2016.

'Mao Tse Tung in an interview with a Hsinhua News Agency correspondent, 29 September 1959', and 'Mao Tse Tung: Quotations from Mao Tse Tung', Chapter 8. People's War', available at https://www.marxists.org/reference/archive/mao/works/red-book/ch08.htm, accessed 20 May, 2019.

'Mao Tse Tung, *On Protracted War*, Selected Works of Mao Tse Tung, May 1938', https://www.marxists.org/reference/archive/mao/selected-works/volume-2/mswv2_09.htm, accessed 20 May 2019.

Sonck, Jean-Pierre, 'Opération Dragon Rouge', available at http://www.congo1960.be/Operation_Dragon_Rouge.htm, accessed 22 May 2019.

Sonck, Jean-Pierre, 'L'Armée privée de Kasongo Nyembo', available at http://www.albertville.be/kasongo-nyembo-01.html, accessed 27 May, 2019.

'The Congo Crisis, 1960-1961, A Critical Oral History Conference', available at https://www.wilsoncenter.org/publication/the-congo-crisis-1960-1961-critical-oral-history-conference, accessed 7 July 2019.

DVD

El Tahri, Jihan, *Cuba: An African Odyssey*, DVD, (Paris: Arte Editions, 2007).

Newspaper articles (by date)

'70 reported dead in Belgian Congo riots', *The Guardian*, 2 November 1959.
Avenir, 21 December 1959.
Echo du Katanga, 20 January 1960.
Le Peuple, 13 February 1960.

'The Congo's 'Quiet Man', Antoine Gizenga', *New York Times*, 15 February, 1960.
Homer Bigart, 'Lumumba Victor in Congo Voting', *New York Times*, 1 June 1960.
'Rhodesia to Bolster Border', *New York Times*, 1 June 1960.
'Belgian Congo Threats Spur European's Exodus', *New York Times*, 2 June 1960.
'Emergency Declared in Katanga', *The Times*, 14 June, 1960.
Harry Gilroy, 'Divisive Efforts Spread in Congo', *New York Times*, 14 June 1960.
'New Congo State to Enforce Unity', *The Times*, 28 June 1960.
'Army to be Commanded by Congolese', *The Times*, 9 July 1960.
'Belgium's Forces Fight Congolese to Quell Risings', *New York Times*, 11 July 1960.
'Polish Arms Ship Sent to Congo', *New York Times*, 17 July 1960.
'New Secession Rejected', *New York Times*, 10 August 1960.
'Congo Troops Fly to Kasai to Stop Secession Effort', *New York Times*, 24 August 1960.
'Mr. Kalonji Flees and Declares war on Mr. Lumumba', *The Times*, 28 August 1960.
'Mr. Lumumba Demands End of Interference', *New York Times*, 9 September 1960.
Henry Tanner, 'Lumumba Bids UN Give Up Controls or Face Ouster', *New York Times*, 9 September 1960.
Henry Tanner, 'Lumumba Staff Men Arrested – Soviet Aides to Leave', *New York Times*, 17 September 1960.
'Stanleyville Troops Mutiny', *New York Times*, 26 October, 1960.
Drew Middleton, 'Reds Said to Spur Efforts in Congo', *New York Times*, 25 November, 1960.
Paul Hoffman, 'Lumumba Backer Escapes Regime', *New York Times*, 27 November, 1960.
Paul Hoffman, 'Pro-Red Lumumba Aide Claims Authority to Rule', *New York Times*, 14 December, 1960.
Paul Hoffman, 'Lumumba Group to Get Arms', *New York Times*, 15 December, 1960.
'OAS Expels Cuba After Delegates Stalk Out', *Chicago Daily Tribune*, 15 February, 1962.
Lloyd Garrison, 'Kalonji, 'King' of South Kasai: Out of Congo Jail', *New York Times*, 9 September 1962.
'Congo Police Mutiny Crushed', *The Canberra Times*, 4 May 1963.
'Report on the Congo: The diamond smugglers' trail crosses the country and nearly everybody is in the racket', *The Atlantic*, Issue of September 1963.
'Cuba Began Role in Zanzibar in '61: Havana's Part in Revolution Outlined in Washington – Guerilla Course Cited', *New York Times*, 2 January, 1964.
Jeune Afrique, numéro 172, 24 February 1964.
'Troops in Congo Fight Ambushers', *New York Times*, 3 May 1964.
'Rebels Seize Congo Town on Border with Burundi', *New York Times*, 18 May, 1964.
'Kivu Rebels Rout Troops of Congo', *New York Times*, 1 June, 1964.
'Rebels Hold in Katanga', *The Times*, 26 June, 1964.
'Fall of Stanleyville to Rebels Reported', *New York Times*, 6 August 1964.
'Men from Many Countries', *The Times*, 23 August 1964.
'Rhodesians Signing Up', *New York Times*, 24 August 1964.
'South Africans Recruited by Congo as Mercenaries', *New York Times*, 24 August 1964.
"Mercenaries' Arrive in Congo', *The Times*, 24 August 1964.
Time Magazine, 27 August 1964.
'The Congo: Help Wanted', *Time*, 4 September 1964.

Lloyd Garrison, 'White Mercenaries Help Retake Key Port in Congo from Rebels', *New York Times*, 8 October, 1964.

Lloyd Garrison, 'Mercenary Group Mutinies in Congo', *New York Times*, 13 October, 1964.

'Congo Rebels May Kill Hostages', *New York Times*, 15 October, 1964.

Lloyd Garrison, 'Tshombe Gains in Battle Against rebels', *New York Times*, 25 October, 1964.

Lloyd Garrison, 'White Mercenaries on a 'Rabbit Hunt', *New York Times Magazine*, 15 November, 1964.

Lloyd Garrison, 'Congolese Find Chinese Ammunition Left by Rebels', *New York Times*, 18 November, 1964.

'Rebel Resistance Light', *New York Times*, 21 November, 1964.

'Rebels in Congo, Near Showdown, Shift Prisoners', *United Press International*, 22 November, 1964.

'10 Britons Brought Back to Safety', *The Times*, 25 November, 1964.

'Africa: The Congo Massacre', *Time*, 4 December, 1964.

'Nos Reporteurs au Congo: La Tragedie des Otages', *Paris Match*, No. 817, 5 décembre 1964.

'Soviet Sees Plot by West in Congo; Tells UN Council Tshombe is Puppet of 'Monopolies – Accuses US Banks', *New York Times*, 18 December, 1964.

'Guevara Receives Rousing Welcome', *Ghanaian Times*, 16 January, 1965.

'Ce jour-là, 24 novembre 1964: nos paras sautent sur Stanleyville', *Paris Match*, RTBF série, 23 August 2003.

Scott Shane, 'Memories of a CIA Officer Resonate in a New Era', *New York Times*, 24 February 2008.

'Victor Dreke Cruz: Cuba's history man still talks of revolution', *The Independent*, 17 April, 2011.

'Congo-Zaïre: l'empire du crime permanent: le massacre de Bakwanga', *Le Phare*, 23 July, 2013.

Nicolas Michel, 'RDC: Léopold II, ce bourreau aux 10 millions de victimes', *L'Echo*, 9 September 2015.

Daniel Boffey, 'Belgium comes to terms with 'human zoos' of its colonial past', *The Guardian*, 16 April 2018.

Notes

Chapter 1

1   "A Manual of Belgian Congo", *Geographical Section of the Naval Intelligence Division*, Naval Staff, Admiralty, (London: His Majesty's Stationery Office, 1891), pp.122-123.

2   Linda Heywood, "Slavery and its Transformation in the Kingdom of the Kongo: 1491-1800", *The Journal of African History*, Vol.50, No.1, p.13.

3   Roland Oliver and Anthony Atmore, *Medieval Africa, 1250-1800* (Cambridge: Cambridge University Press, 2001), p.173.

4   Marcel Soret, *Les Kongo Nord-Occidentaux* (Paris: L'Harmattan, 1959), p.21, in Verhaegen, *L'ABAKO et l'indépendance du Congo belge: dix ans de nationalisme kongo* (Paris: L'Harmattan, 2003), p.19.

5   Frank T. Kryza, *The Race for Timbuktu: In Search of Africa's City of Gold* (New York: Harper Collins, 2006), p.11.

6   David Livingstone, *The Last Journals of David Livingstone in Central Africa*, (New York: Harper and Brothers Limited, 1875).

7   Daniel Crawford, *Thinking Black: 22 Years without a Break in the Long Grass*, (George H. Doran: New York, 1912), p.15.

8   Arm Bethune, *Le Katanga, Province Belge*, (Paris: Broché, 2010), p.72.

9   Situated between the Democratic Republic of the Congo and Zambia.

10 Nicolas Michel, "RDC: Léopold II, ce bourreau aux 10 millions de victimes", *L'Echo*, 9 September 2015.

11 "Republic of the Congo (Léopoldville), The Province of the Katanga and Congolese Independence", *Document Division of the Ministry of Foreign Affairs*, Number 1, January, 1962.

12 R. Brion and J-L Moreau, *De la mine à Mars: La Genèse d'Umicore*, (Brussels: Lannoo, 2006), p.69 as quoted in "Les Géants du Cuivre: Leçons tirées des Entreprises Etatiques Minières en RDC et en Zambie", *Natural Resource Governance Institute*, undated, p.15, https://www.resourcegovernance.org/sites/default/files/documents/nrgi_nmc_french.pdf, accessed April 2017.

13 Robert Harms, "The End of Red Rubber: A Reassessment", *The Journal of African History*, Volume 16, Issue 1, January 1975, pp.73–88.

14 William J. Samarin, *The Black Man's Burden: African Colonial Labor on the Congo and Ubangi Rivers, 1880-1900* (Boulder: Westview Press, 1989), p.119.

15 Leo Zeilig, David Renton, and David Seddon, *The Congo: Plunder and Resistance* (London: Zed Books, 2007), p.38.

16 Ruth M. Slade, "King Leopold's Congo: Aspects of the Development of Race Relations in the Congo Independent State", *Institute of Race Relations* (Oxford: OUP, 1962), p.177.

17 Harold St. John Lloyd Winterbottom, et al., *The Belgian Congo* (Great Britain: Naval Intelligence Division, 1944), p.200.

18 Peter Abbot, *Armies in East Africa* (Oxford: Osprey Publishing, 2002), p.10.

19 *The Belgian Congo*, p.201.

20 Crawford Young, *Politics in Congo: Decolonization and Independence* (Oxford: OUP, 1965), p.441.

21 Young, *Politics in the Congo: Decolonization and Independence*, p.441.

22 Henry Richard Fox Bourne, *Civilisation in Congoland, a Story of International Wrong-Doing*, (London: P.S King & son, 1903), p.89.

23 Winterbottom, et al., *The Belgian Congo*, p.207.

24 René Cornet, *La bataille du rail* (Brussels: Editions L. Cuypers, 1953) p.336, in Verhaegen, *ABAKO: 1950-1960* (Brussels: CRISP, 1962), p.20.

25 Winterbottom, et al., *The Belgian Congo*, p.239.

26 "Louis Marie François Frank", *Biographie Coloniale Belge*, Institut Royale de la colonie belge, Tome III, 1952, pp.325-343.

27 National Society for the Study of Air Transport.

28 Winterbottom, et al., *The Belgian Congo*, pp.240-241.

29 Winterbottom, et al., *The Belgian Congo*, pp.240-241.

30 Winterbottom, et al., *The Belgian Congo*, pp.235.

31 Georges Brausch, *Belgian Administration in the Congo* (Oxford: OUP, 1961), p.11.

32 Brausch, *Belgian Administration in the Congo*, p.2.

33 International Labour Office, "Rapport sur les salaires dans la République du Congo" (Geneva, 1960), p.12, in Brausch, *Belgian Administration in the Congo*, p.2.

34 Some sources put this figure at $25 per month. See, Crawford Young, "Background to Independence", *Transition*, No.25, 1966, p.36.

35 "Les problèmes du travail en Afrique" (Geneva: International Labour Office, 1959), p.18.

36 Brausch, *Belgian Administration in the Congo*, p.15.

37 Brausch, *Belgian Administration in the Congo*, p.20.

Chapter 2

1. Louis-François Vanderstraeten, La *répression de la révolte des Pende du Kwango en 1931* (Brussels: Académie Royale des Sciences d'Outre-mer, 2001), p.78.
2. Zeilig, Renton, and Seddon, *The Congo: Plunder and Resistance*, p.69.
3. Zeilig, Renton, and Seddon, *The Congo: Plunder and Resistance*, p.69.
4. Bogumil Jewsiewicki, Kilola Lema, Jean-Luc Vellut, "Documents pour servir de l'histoire sociale du Zaire: grèves dans le Bas-Congo en 1945", *Etudes d'histoire africaine*, 1973, pp.155-188.
5. Crawford Young, *Politics in the Congo: Decolonization and Independence* (New Jersey: Princeton University Press, 2015) pp.292-293.
6. Other associations were the *Union desAnciens Elèves des Frères Maristes* (UNELMA); the *Association des Anciens Elèves desFrères Chrètiens* (ASSANEF); and the *Anciens Elèves des Pères Jésuites*.
7. The term is used in its loosest sense. Anyone who could read and write was deemed to be an academic.
8. Harold D. Weaver Jr, "Paul Robeson and the Pan-African World", *Présence Africaine*, No.107, 3 trimester, 1978, pp.218-219.
9. This association provided *évolués* with the means of discussing working conditions and wages. Ultimately, discussions would turn to equal pay for equal work and discrimination in the workplace. See, Colin Legum, "The Belgian Congo: Revolt of the Elite", *Africa South*, Vol.4, No.1, October-December 1959, pp.105-106.
10. Yolanda Covington-Ward, "Joseph Kasa-Vubu, ABAKO? and Performances of Kongo Nationalism in the Independence of Congo", *Journal of Black Studies*, Special issue: 1960s Africa in Historical Perspective, Vol.43, No.1, January 2012, p.74.
11. Rene Lemarchand, "The Bases of Nationalism among the Bakongo", *Africa: Journal of the International African Institute*, Vol.31, No.4, October 1961, p.346.
12. A. A. J. Van Bilsen, *Vers l'indépendance du Congo et du Ruanda-Urundi*, (Kinshasa : Presses Universitaires, 1977), p.296.
13. "Excerpts from Prof. Van Bilsen's "Thirty Year Plan", in "Conflict in the Congo", *Africa Today*, Vol.7, No.5, September 1960, p.5.
14. "Excerpts from Prof. Van Bilsen's "Thirty Year Plan", p.5.
15. Jean Labrique, *Congo politique* (Leopoldville: Editions de l'Avenir, 1957), pp.251-264.
16. Benoît Verhaegen, *ABAKO, 1950-1960* (Brussels: Documents du CRISP, 1962), pp.37-44.
17. Verhaegen, *ABAKO, 1950-1960*, pp.37-44.
18. William Edward Burghardt Du Bois, "Fifth Pan-African Congress final resolution", October 1945, W. E. B. Du Bois Papers (MS 312). Special Collections and University Archives, University of Massachusetts Amherst Libraries.
19. Emmanuel Kwaku Akeampong and Henry Louis Gates, Dictionary of African Biography (New York: OUP, 2012), p.526.
20. Akeampongand Gates, *Dictionary of African Biography*, p.526.
21. George M. Houser, "A Report on the All African People's Conference Held in Accra, Ghana, December 8-13, 1958", *American Committee on Africa*, New York.
22. Patrice Lumumba, "Speech at Accra", available at https://www.blackpast.org/global-african-history/1958-patrice-lumumba-speech-accra/, accessed 14 May 2019.
23. Patrice Lumumba, "Speech at Accra".
24. Patrice Lumumba, "Speech at Accra".
25. Patrice Lumumba, "Speech at Accra".
26. The CEREA sought the unity of the Kivu people and the CONAKAT was restricted to activities in Katanga.
27. Georges Nzongola-Ntalaja, *From Leopold to Kabila: A People's History* (London: Zed Books, 2002), pp.84-86.
28. Leo Zeilig, *Lumumba: Africa's Lost Leader* (London: Haus, 2008), p.70.
29. Colin Legum, *Congo Disaster* (Baltimore: Penguin Books, 1960), p.59.
30. "70 reported dead in Belgian Congo riots", *The Guardian*, 2 November 1959.
31. A. Rubbens, "Political Awakening in the Congo", *Civilisations*, Vol.10, No.1, 1960, p.64.
32. Rubbens, "Political Awakening in the Congo", p.74.
33. Jeanne M. Haskin, *The Tragic State of the Congo: from Decolonization to Dictatorship* (New York: Algora Publishing, 2005), pp.19-20.
34. Homer Bigart, "Lumumba Victor in Congo Voting", *New York Times*, 1 June 1960.
35. "Belgian Congo Threats Spur European's Exodus", *New York Times*, 2 June 1960.
36. "Rhodesia to Bolster Border", *New York Times*, 1 June 1960.
37. "Emergency Declared in Katanga", *The Times*, 14 June, 1960.
38. Harry Gilroy, "Divisive Efforts Spread in Congo", *New York Times*, 14 June 1960.
39. "Tshombe, Moïse-Kapenda", *Biographie Belge d'Outre-Mer* (Brussels: Académie Royale des Sciences d'Outre-mer, Tome VII-A), pp.462-476.
40. Article 250 of the Fundamental Law of 19 May 1960.
41. "New Congo State to Enforce Unity", *The Times*, 28 June 1960.
42. Madeleine Kalb, *The Congo Cables: The Cold War in Africa-From Eisenhower to Kennedy* (London: Macmillan, 1982), p.3.

Chapter 3

1. Jihan El Tahri, *Cuba: An African Odyssey*, DVD, (Paris: Arte Editions, 2007), 4.06.
2. Ludo de Witte, *The Assassination of Lumumba* (Brussels: Karthala, 2000), p.36.
3. "Patrice Lumumba, First Prime Minister of the Congo, June 30, 1960", https://africanlegends.files.wordpress.com/2011/06/patrice-lumumba-speech.pdf, accessed 6 September 2016.
4. El Tahri,*Cuba: An African Odyssey.*
5. Guy Vanthemsche, *Belgium and the* Congo (Cambridge: Cambridge University Press, 201), p.254.
6. Robert B. Edgerton, *The Troubled Heart of Africa: A History of the Congo* (St. Martin's Press: New York, 2002), p.186.
7. Edgerton, *The Troubled Heart of Africa: A History of the Congo*, p.186.
8. Nzongola-Ntalaja, *The Congo from Leopold to Kabila: A People's History*, p.67.
9. Edgerton, *The Troubled Heart of Africa: A History of the Congo*, p.189.
10. "Army to be Commanded by Congolese", *The Times*, 9 July 1960.
11. Larry Devlin, *Chief of Station, Congo* (New York: Public Affairs, 2008), introduction, xiii-xv.
12. Edgerton, *The Troubled Heart of Africa: A History of the Congo*, p.188.
13. "Belgium's Forces Fight Congolese to Quell Risings", *New York Times*, 11 July 1960.
14. Anicet Kashamura, *De Lumumba aux colonels*, (Paris: Broché, 1966), pp.96-97, as quoted in Kalb, *Congo Cables*, p.7.
15. "US Mission at the UN", Cable No.1137 to the State Department in Kalb, *Congo Cables*, p.15.
16. "Questions relating to the situation in the Republic of the Congo (Leopoldville)", The Yearbook of the United Nations, 1960, Part 1, Chapter VII, p.52.
17. "Questions relating to the situation in the Republic of the Congo (Leopoldville)", p.54.
18. *New York Times*, 29 July 1960, in Kalb, *Congo Cables*, p.19.
19. Daniel L. Haulman, "Congolese Mercy Airlift", *Air Mobility Command Museum*, (date unknown) available at https://amcmuseum.org/history/congolese-mercy-airlift/, accessed 1 July 2019.
20. Kalb, *Congo Cables*, p.19.
21. Paul Collier and Nicholas Sambanis (eds.) *Understanding Civil War (Volume 1: Africa) Evidence and Analysis* (World Bank: 2005), p.67.
22. Nzongola-Ntalaja, *From Leopold to Kabila: A People's History*, p.104.

23. Nzongola-Ntalaja, *From Leopold to Kabila: A People's History*, p.104.
24. "New Secession Rejected", *New York Times*, 10 August 1960.
25. Godfrey Mwakikagile, *Africa, 1960-1970: Chronicle and Analysis* (Dar Es Salaam: New Africa Press, 2014), p.37.
26. Patrice Lumumba, "Speech given at the Congress for the Freedom of Culture", Ibadan, Nigeria, March 22, 1959, available at https://www.marxists.org/subject/africa/lumumba/1960/08/25.htm, accessed 20 June 2019.
27. "From a letter to Dag Hammarskjöld, U.N. Secretary-General, August 14, 1960", https://www.marxists.org/subject/africa/lumumba/1960/08/umgensec.htm, accessed 27 January 2015.
28. Eric S. Packham, *Freedom and Anarchy*, (Nova Science Publishers, Inc.: 1996), p.54.
29. "Polish Arms Ship Sent to Congo", *New York Times*, 17 July 1960.
30. "US Mission at the United Nations Cable", Nos. 560 and "US Mission at the United Nations Cable", Nos. 560. 69.
31. "Congo Troops Fly to Kasai to Stop Secession Effort", *New York Times*, 24 August 1960.
32. "Mr. Kalonji Flees and Declares war on Mr. Lumumba", *The Times*, 28 August 1960.
33. Albert Kalonji Mulopwe, *Dossier du massacre des Baluba à Bakwanga de 1960* (Kinshasa: Conférence nationale souveraine, 1992), p.8.
34. "Congo-Zaïre: l'empire du crime permanent: le massacre de Bakwanga", *Le Phare*, 23 July, 2013.
35. Peter Scholl-Latour, *Mort sur le grand fleuve. Du Congo au Zaïre, chronique d'une indépendance* (Paris: Presses de la Cité, 1988), p.200.
36. Lloyd Garrison, "Kalonji, 'King' of South Kasai: Out of Congo Jail", *New York Times*, 9 September 1962.
37. Eric S. Packham, *Freedom and Anarchy*, p.71.
38. Young, *Politics in the Congo: Decolonization and Independence*, p.454.
39. Jean-Claude Willame, *Patrimonialism and Political Change in the Congo* (Stanford: Stanford University Press, 1972), p.67.
40. Nzongola-Ntalaja, *From Leopold to Kabila: A People's History*, p.107.
41. Paul Nugent, *Africa since Independence: a Comparative History* (New York: Palgrave-Macmillan, 2004), p.86.
42. Nugent, *Africa since Independence: a Comparative History*, p.97.
43. Garrison, "Kalonji, 'King' of South Kasai: Out of Congo Jail", *New York Times*, 9 September 1962.
44. Packham, *Freedom and Anarchy*, p.66.
45. Daniel L. Haulman, "Crisis in the Congo: Operation New Tape", pp.24-25, in Timothy Warnock (ed.), *Short of War: Major USAF Contingency Operations*, Air Force History and Museums Program, 2000.
46. "Telegram from the Embassy in the Congo to the Department of State", August 29 1960, FRUS, Vol. XXIII, D192.
47. Nzongola-Ntalaja, *From Leopold to Kabila: A People's History*, p.108.
48. Nzongola-Ntalaja, *From Leopold to Kabila: A People's History*, p.108.
49. Nzongola-Ntalaja, *From Leopold to Kabila: A People's History*, p.108.
50. Jules Gérard-Libois and Benoît Verhaegen, *Congo 1960*, Tome 2, (Brussels: CRISP, 1963), pp.828-850, as quoted in Kalb, *Congo Cables*, p.75.
51. "Mr. Lumumba Demands End of Interference", *New York Times*, 9 September 1960.
52. Henry Tanner, "Lumumba Bids UN Give Up Controls or Face Ouster", *New York Times*, 9 September 1960.
53. Devlin, *Chief of Station, Congo*, pp.76-77.
54. Devlin, *Chief of Station, Congo*, p.78.
55. Gerald Horne, *Mau Mau in Harlem?: The US and the Liberation of Kenya*, (New York: Palgrave Macmillan, 2009), p.3.
56. Foreign Relations of the United States, Vol. XXIII, *Congo, 1960-1968*, (Washington: United States Government Printing Office, 2013), introduction.
57. Devlin, *Chief of Station, Congo*, p.9.
58. CIA Cable, "Leopoldville to Director", 18 August 1960, FRUS, Vol. XXIII, Congo, D421.
59. "Alleged Assassination Plots Involving Foreign Leaders", US Senate Select Committee to Study Governmental Operations (Washington D.C.: US Government Printing Office, 1975) p.18.
60. "*National Security Council Meeting*" Washington, 25 July 1960, Central Intelligence Agency Files, Job 79R00890A, Box 13, Folder 1, NSC Briefings, July 1960. Top Secret; [*codeword not declassified*].
61. Tim Weiner, *Legacy of the Ashes: The History of the CIA* (London: Penguin Books, 2007), p.162.
62. CIA Cable, "Leopoldville to Director".
63. A number of works contradict these perceptions of Lumumba. Although not entirely at ease with Lumumba's political leanings, they saluted his stand against what was considered as continuing Belgian exploitation of the Congo. Lumumba's struggle for Congolese unity and his refusal to accept independence with "strings attached" made him somewhat of a martyr and even a 'saviour' of Africa in the eyes of some. See, James Hunter Meriwether, *Proudly We Can be Africans, Black Americans and Africa, 1935-1961*, (North Carolina: University of North Carolina Press, 2002), p.233. For further analysis of how black Americans related to Africa's fight for independence see, James Hunter Meriwether, *The African Connection and the Struggle for Freedom: Africa's Role in American Life* (Los Angeles: University of California, 1995).
64. This plan was outlined in a cable sent to Larry Devlin by Bronson Tweedy, the Chief of the Africa Division of the CIA's clandestine services. CIA Cable, "Leopoldville to Director".
65. CIA Cable, "Leopoldville to Director", 24 August 1960, FRUS, Vol. XXIII, Congo, D427.
66. CIA Cable, "Leopoldville to Director", D427.
67. Henry Tanner, "Lumumba Staff Men Arrested – Soviet Aides to Leave", *New York Times*, 17 September 1960.
68. Mpolo and Vice President of the Congolese senate Joseph Okito were killed alongside Lumumba in Katanga.
69. CIA Cable, "Leopoldville to Director", 15 August 1960, FRUS, Vol. XXIII, Congo, D419.
70. "Alleged Assassination Plots Involving Foreign Leaders", p.19.
71. In reality, this was Sidney Gottlieb. See Kalb, *Congo Cables*, p.102.
72. Devlin, *Chief of Station, Congo*, p.95.
73. "Alleged Assassination Plots Involving Foreign Leaders", p.21.
74. Devlin, *Chief of Station, Congo*, p.95.
75. Scott Shane, "Memories of a CIA Officer Resonate in a New Era", *New York Times*, 24 February 2008.
76. Kalb, *Congo Cables*, p.159.
77. Kalb, *Congo Cables*, pp.184-186.

Chapter 4
1. "The Congo's 'Quiet Man', Antoine Gizenga", *New York Times*, 15 February, 1960.
2. Kalb, *Congo Cables*, p.14.
3. Kalb, *Congo Cables*, p.14.
4. "Report on Alleged Assassination Plots of Foreign Leaders", p.18.
5. "Stanleyville Troops Mutiny", *New York Times*, 26 October 1960.
6. Paul Hoffman, "Lumumba Backer Escapes Regime", *New York Times*, 27 November 1960.
7. Kalb, *Congo Cables*, p.166.
8. Paul Hoffman, "Pro-Red Lumumba Aide Claims Authority to Rule", *New York Times*, 14 December 1960.
9. Drew Middleton, "Reds Said to Spur Efforts in Congo", *New York Times*, 25 November 1960.
10. Paul Hoffman, "Lumumba Group to Get Arms", *New York Times*, 15 December 1960.
11. Kalb, *Congo Cables*, p.172.

12 Sergei Mazov, "Soviet Aid to the Gizenga Government in the Former Belgian Congo (1960-61) as Reflected in Russian Archives", *Cold War History*, Vol. 7, No. 3, August 2007, p.6.
13 Christopher Othen, *Katanga 1960-63: Mercenaries, Spies and the African Nation that Waged War on the World* (The History Press, 2015), p.91.
14 This amounts to around 2-6 million Congolese francs. See, "Transcript of the talk between Deputy of Foreign Minister of the USSR V. V. Kuznetsov and Minister of Education and Arts of the Republic of Congo, Pierre Mulele, 8 March 1961", as quoted in Mazov, "Soviet Aid to the Gizenga Government in the Former Belgian Congo (1960-61) as Reflected in Russian Archives", p.433.
15 "The Congo Crisis, 1960-1961, A Critical Oral History Conference", p.38, available at https://www.wilsoncenter.org/publication/the-congo-crisis-1960-1961-critical-oral-history-conference, consulted 7 July 2019.
16 "Special National Intelligence Estimate 65-61", FRUS 1961-1963, Washington, 10 January 1961, Document 2.
17 "Telegram from the Embassy in the Congo to the Department of State", 10 January 1961, FRUS, Vol. XXI, Africa, D3.
18 Manano is a town situated deep in the jungles of North Kivu in the east of the country. It is endowed with a mine containing some of the richest deposits of tin in the world. It was also the seat of the "Government of Lualaba" set up by provincial governor and another Lumumbist, Prosper Mwamba-Ilunga.
19 "Memorandum of Conversation", Washington, 26 January 1961, FRUS, Vol.XXI, Africa, D11.
20 Jaques Lantier, *Le temps des mercenaires* (Paris: CAL, 1969), p.125.
21 Kalb, *Congo Cables*, p.175.
22 "Briefing Paper Prepared in the Department of State", Washington, undated, FRUS 1961-1963, D7.
23 Kalb, *Congo Cables*, p.177.
24 Young, *Politics in the Congo*, (2015), p.331.
25 "Memorandum from Williams to Rusk", 7 February 1961, Dept. of State, NSC Files, Lot 70, D265.
26 Gérard-Libois, *Secession au Katanga* (Brussels: CRISP, 1963), p.163.
27 Jaques Lantier, *Le temps des mercenaires* (Paris: CAL, 1969) p.126.
28 Conor Cruise O'Brien, *To Katanga and Back* (London: Four Square Books, 1965) p.160.
29 "UN Security Council Resolution 161" [The Congo Question] UN Security Council, 21 February 1961.
30 Kalb, *Congo Cables*, p.243.
31 "US Consulate in Elisabethville Cable No.576 to US State Department", 3 January 1961, in Kalb, *Congo Cables*, p.243.
32 "US Embassy in Leopoldville Cable No.1835 to US State Department", 3 February 1961, in Kalb, *Congo Cables*, p.243.
33 "US Embassy in Leopoldville Cable No.1847 to US State Department", 3 April 1961, in Kalb, *Congo Cables*, p.245.
34 Benoit Verhaegen, *Congo 1961* (Brussels: CRISP, 1962), p.47.
35 Mazov, "Soviet Aid to the Gizenga Government in the Former Belgian Congo (1960-61) as Reflected in Russian Archives", p.431.
36 "Memorandum of Conversation", Washington, 8 March 1961, FRUS, Vol.XXI, Africa, D225.
37 "Brezhnev's trip to the Republic of Guinea, Ghana and Morocco", 24 February 1961, AVP RF, Collection 0601, Folder 4, File 9, p.6, in Mazov, "Soviet Aid to the Gizenga Government in the Former Belgian Congo (1960-61) as Reflected in Russian Archives", p.431.
38 "The Volta River and Related Projects", Washington, 17 February 1961, FRUS, Vol.XXI, Africa, D223.
39 "Questions Concerning the Situation in the Republic of the Congo (Leopoldville)", Chapter VII, pp.60-61, available at https://www.un.org/Depts/dhl/dag/docs/congo61.pdf, accessed 21 May 2019.

Chapter 5

1 M.H. Buttgenbach, *Les mines du Katanga* (Brussels: Imprimerie A. Lesigne, 1908), pp.5-6.
2 William A. Hance, and Irene S. Van Dongen, "The Port of Lobito and the Benguela Railway", *Geographical Review*, Vol.46, No.4, October 1956, pp.460-487.
3 "The Province of Katanga and Congolese Independence", Republic of the Congo (Leopoldville), Document Division of the Ministry of Foreign Affairs, No.1, January 1962, p.5.
4 Other sources put this number at 1,709,659. See, Rene Lemarchand, "The Limits of Self-Determination: The Case of the Katanga Secession", *The American Political Science Review*, Vol.56, No.2, June 1962, p.405.
5 Daniel J. Crowley, "Politics and Tribalism in the Katanga", *The Western Political Quarterly*, Vol.16, No.1, March 1963, p.69.
6 Jean-Luc Vellut, "Mining in the Belgian Congo", 28, in David Birmingham and Phyllis M. Martin (eds), *History of Central Africa* (New York and London: Longman, 1983). Quoted in Erik Kennes and Miles Larmer, *The Katangese Gendarmes and War in Central Africa: Fighting their Way Home* (Bloomington: Indiana University Press, 2016), p.31.
7 J. Comhaire, "Some Aspects of Urbanization in the Belgian Congo", *American Journal of Sociology*, No.42, July 1956, pp.11-13.
8 Comhaire, "Some Aspects of Urbanization in the Belgian Congo", pp.11-13.
9 Two other types of urban unit were created in 1957: the *commune* was administered by a burgomaster assisted by a municipal council, and the *ville* was a larger urban area comprising several *communes*. Leopoldville and Elisabethville were both *villes*.
10 Brausch, *Belgian Administration in the Congo*, p.48.
11 Similar elections were held in Bakuvu, Stanleyville and Luluabourg in 1958.
12 Slade, *King Leopold's Congo: Aspects of the Development of Race Relations in the Congo Independent State*, p.25.
13 Olga Boone, Carte ethnique du Congo: quart sud-est (Tervuern, Royal Museum for Central Africa, 1961) in J. Hiernaux, "Luba du katanga et Luba du Kasai (Congo): comparaison de deux populations de même origine", *Bulletins et Mémoires de la Société d'Anthropologie de Paris*, 1964, p.621.
14 Hiernaux, "Luba du katanga et Luba du Kasai (Congo): comparaison de deux populations de même origine", p.613.
15 "The Province of Katanga and Congolese Independence", p.5.
16 At its origin, the CONAKAT also included representations from the following ethnic and tribal groups: the *Association des Bahemba de Kongolo* (ASSOBAKO); the *Association des Batabwa ou Bena Marungu du Katanga* (BBK); the *Association des Basonge du Katanga* (ASSOBAKAT); the *Association des Originaires du Luapala Moero Katanga* (ALMOKAT); the *Association des Tshokwe du Katanga et de Rhodésie* (AKTAR), the *Union des Bwami des Basumbwa-Bayeke* (UBWAKA), and the *Fédération des Tribus du Haut-Katanga* (FETRIKAT). The confederation also included Jason Sendwe's BALUBAKAT.
17 "The Province of Katanga and Congolese Independence", p.4.
18 "Moïse-Kapende Tshombé", *Académie Royale des Sciences d'Outre-Mer*, Biographie Belge d'Outre-Mer, Tome VII-A, Col. 462-476.
19 Romain Yakemtchouk, "Aux origines du séparatisme katangais", Académie Royale des Sciences d'Outre-Mer, Classe des Sciences Morales et Politiques, *Mémoires in-8*, Nouvelle Série, Tome 50, Fasc. 1, Brussels, 1988, p.88.
20 "Les problèmes au Katanga", *Courrier hebdomadaire du CRISP*, Vol.55, No.9, 1960, pp.1-19.
21 Fédération des associations tribales de la province de Kasaï.
22 This was not a political party as such. It was a tribal organisation representing the Chokwe of the Congo, Angola and Rhodesia.
23 *Echo du Katanga*, 20 January 1960, in *Courrier hebdomadaire du CRISP*, p.6.
24 *Avenir*, 21 December 1959, in *Courrier hebdomadaire du CRISP*, p.6.

25 *Courrier hebdomadaire du CRISP*, p.8.
26 *Courrier hebdomadaire du CRISP*, p.8.
27 *Courrier hebdomadaire du CRISP*, p.14.
28 "Republic of the Congo: The Province of Katanga and Congolese Independence", p.6.
29 *Le Peuple*, 13 February 1960, in *Courrier hebdomadaire du CRISP*, p.5.
30 Romain Pasteger, *Le Visage des affreux* mercenaires Katangais, (Paris: Broché, 2004), p.6.
31 Kennes and Larmer, *The Katangese Gendarmes and War in Central Africa: Fighting their Way Home*, p.38.
32 Colin Gonze, "Katanga Secession: The New Colonialism", *Africa Today*, Vol.9, No.1, February 1962, p.6.
33 Gonze, "Katanga Secession: The New Colonialism", p.6.
34 "Loi fondamentale sur la structure de l'Etat du Congo belge", May 1960, https://leganet.cd/Legislation/Droit%20Public/Loi%20fondamentale%201960.pdf, accessed 24 May 2019.
35 "Republic of the Congo: The Province of Katanga and Congolese Independence", p.12.
36 "Republic of the Congo: The Province of Katanga and Congolese Independence", p.16.
37 "Republic of the Congo: The Province of Katanga and Congolese Independence", p.18.
38 "Republic of the Congo: The Province of Katanga and Congolese Independence", p.20.
39 "Republic of the Congo: The Province of Katanga and Congolese Independence", pp.19-21.
40 Luc De Vos, Emmanuel Gérard, Jules Gérard-Libois, and Philippe Raxhorn, *Les secrets de l'affaire Lumumba* (Bruxelles: Editions Racine, 2005), p.62.
41 "Republic of the Congo: The Province of Katanga and Congolese Independence", p.26.
42 Miles Larmer, "Of Local Identities and Transnational Conflict: the Katangese Gendarmes and Central-Southern Africa's Forty-year war, 1960-1999", in Nir Arielli and Bruce Collins (eds.), *Transnational Soldiers: Foreign Military Enlistment in the Modern Era* (London: Palgrave Macmillan, 2013), p.164.
43 Jean-Pierre Sonck, "L'Armée privée de Kasongo Nyembo", available at http://www.albertville.be/kasongo-nyembo-01.html, accessed 27 May 2017.
44 Catherine Hoskyns, *The Congo since Independence: January 1960-December 1961*, (New York: Oxford University Press, 1965), p.142, quoted in J.J.G. Clarke, "The Congo Mercenary: A History and Analysis", *The South African Institute of International Affairs*, Johannesburg, 1968, p.21.
45 Colin Gonze, "Katanga Secession: The New Colonialism", p.6.
46 Zumbach was a World War Two fighter pilot who had flown with the 303rd Polish Fighter Squadron of the Royal Air Force (RAF). Later, Zumbach's career in aviation would continue as a member of the Biafran Air Force (BAF), see Philip Jowett, *Modern African Wars: The Nigerian-Biafran War*, (London: Osprey Publishing, 2016), p.67.
47 Jeremiah Cornelius Puren joined the South African Air Force (SAAF) as a navigator during WWII and flew on missions over North Africa and the Middle East. After the war, he joined the Royal Air Force and in March 1961 was contacted by Charles Huyghe. After expulsion from the Congo Puren took part in a failed attempt to overthrow the government of the Seychelles (see, "Report of the Security Council Commission of Inquiry Established under Resolution 496 (1981)", Security Council Official Records, United Nations, 1982) and, in 1986, he wrote his memoirs, see, Jerry Puren and Brian Pottinger, *Mercenary Commander*, (South Africa: Galago Publishing, 1986). This work has not been used due to its unreliability as a source.
48 David Shaftel, "The Black Eagle of Harlem", *Air & Space Magazine*, December 2008.
49 The choice to advertise in Toulouse was due to the city's long-held links to the aviation industry. See "Nations Unies, Conseil de Sécurité", Document S/5053/Add.12, 8 octobre 1962.
50 "L'Aviation Militaire Katangaise 1960-1963" in, "Les Vieilles Tiges de Belgique", Périodique trimestriel, juillet-août-spetembre, No.3/97.
51 For a complete list of aircraft used by the FAK see, Victor Flintham, *Air Wars and Aircraft: A Detailed Record of Air Combat, 1945 to the Present* (New York: Facts on File, 1990), p.107.
52 Document S/5053/Add.12, 8 octobre 1962, op.cit.
53 The three Fouga Magisters arrived in Katanga in February 1961. See, A. Walter Dorn, "The UN's First 'Air Force': Peacekeepers in Combat, Congo 1960-64", *Journal of Military History*, Vol. 77, no.4 (October 2013), 1399-1425.
54 "L'Aviation Militaire Katangaise 1960-1963", op.cit.
55 "L'Aviation Militaire Katangaise 1960-1963", op.cit.
56 Victor Flintham, *Air Wars and Aircraft: A Detailed Record of Air Combat, 1945 to the Present* (New York: Facts on File, 1990), p.107.
57 Pasteger, *Le Visage des affreuxmercenaires Katangais*, pp.11-13.
58 Pasteger, *Le Visage des affreuxmercenaires Katangais*, p.15.
59 Othen, *Katanga, 1960-1963: Mercenaries, Spies and the African Nation that waged War on the World*, p.82.
60 S.J.G. Clarke, "The Congo Mercenary: A History and Analysis", *SAIII*, Johannesburg, 1968, p.23.
61 Pasteger, *Le Visage des affreuxmercenaires Katangais*, p.19.
62 Jean-Pierre Sonck, "Forces de l'ordre et Sûreté Katanga 1960-1961 ", 1998, p.21.
63 "Livre blanc du Gouvernement katangais sur les activités des hors-la-loi dans certains territoires baluba" (Elisabethville: Gouvernement katangais, 1961), pp.27-29.
64 Célestin Kabuya Lumuna Sando, *Nord-Katanga 1960-1964. De la Sécession à la guerre civile. Le meurtre des chefs* (Paris: L'Harmattan, 1992), p.74.
65 Kabuya Lumuna Sando, *Nord-Katanga 1960-1964. De la Sécession à la guerre civile. Le meurtre des chefs*, p.74.
66 Verhaegen, *Congo 1961* (Brussels: Les Dossiers du CRISP, 1962), p.774.
67 Thomas Banjikila, *Epuration ethnique en Afrique*: les "Kasaians", Katanga 1961-Shaba 1992 (Paris: L'Harmattan, 1997), p.115.
68 Jules Gérard-Libois and Benoit Verhaegen, *Congo 1960*, (Brussels: Dossiers du CRISP, 1961), pp.173-174, as quoted in Clark, "The Congo Mercenary: A History and Analysis", p.25.
69 This name is believed to have been given to mercenaries at the end of September 1960. Colonel Crevecoeur, then chief of the Katanganese Gendarmes was reportedly looking over the CVs of those soldiers of fortune being sent to him. On seeing that many had criminal records and/or held sympathies with Nazi Germany, Crevecoeur stated that these were not soldiers, they were "frightening". See, Pasteger, *Le Visage des affreuxmercenaires Katangais*, p.25.
70 Othen, *Katanga, 1960-1963: Mercenaries, Spies and the African Nation that waged War on the World*, p.91.
71 Jules Gérard-Libois, *Secession au Katanga* (Brussels: CRISP, 1963), p.192.
72 Colonel E.R. Vandewalle, *L'Ommegang : Odyssée & Reconquête de Stanleyville, 1964* (Brussels: Le Livre Africain, 1970), pp.15-16.
73 Ludo de Witte, *L'Assassinat de Lumumba*, (Paris: Broché, 2000), p.175.
74 Jaques Duchemin, Jaques Le Bailly, and Roger Trinquier, *Notre guerre au Katanga* (Paris: Editions de la pensée moderne, 1963), p.53.
75 Anthony Mockler, *Mercenaries,* (London: Macdonald, 1969), p.159.
76 Roger Trinquier, *Modern Warfare: A French View of Counterinsurgency* (London and Dunmow: Pall Mall Press, 1964). First published by Editions de la Table Ronde, Paris in 1961 under the title *La Guerre Moderne*.

77 Duchemin, Le Bailly, and Trinquier, *Notre guerre au Katanga*, pp.56-64.
78 Written correspondence with Nigel Osborn, May 2015.
79 Mike Hoare, *The Road to Kalamata: A Congo Mercenary's Personal Memoir* (Boulder, CO: Paladin Press, 1989), p.5.

Chapter 6

1 Led by United States Army officer Colonel M.J.L. Greene, from July 1962 a Special Military Advisory Team recommended that the Congo's armed forces should be modernised and receive training under the authority of the UN.
2 "Loi du 14 août 1962 sur la création des provinces de Kwango, Kwilu et Mai-Ndombe", available at www.droitcongolais.info, accessed 20 April 2019.
3 Benoit Verhaegen, *Mulele et la révolution populaire au Kwilu* (Paris: L'Harmattan, 2006), p.17.
4 Henri Nicolaï, "Naissance d'une région en Afrique centrale: Le Kwilu", *Les Cahiers d'Outre-Mer*, 1964, pp.292-313.
5 Nicolaï, "Naissance d'une région en Afrique centrale: Le Kwilu", p.298.
6 Verhaegen, *Mulele et la révolution populaire au Kwilu*, p.23.
7 Verhaegen, *Mulele et la révolution populaire au Kwilu*, p.296.
8 Ludo Martens, *Pierre Mulele, ou, La seconde vie de Lumumba* (Brussels: EPO, 1985), p.30.
9 Martens, *Pierre Mulele, ou, La seconde vie de Lumumba*, p.271.
10 Renee C. Fox, Willy de Craemer and Jean-Marie Ribeaucourt, "The Second Independence": A Case Study of the Kwilu Rebellion in the Congo", *Comparative Studies in Society and History*, Vol.8, No.1, October 1965, p.96.
11 Fox et al.,"The Second Independence": A Case Study of the Kwilu Rebellion in the Congo", p.22.
12 Théophile Bula-Bula, *Pierre Mulele et le maquis du Kwilu en R.D. Congo* (Paris: L'Harmattan, 2010), pp.13-14.
13 Bruce S. Fetter, "The Luluabourg Revolt at Elisabethville", *African Historical Studies*, Vol. 2, No. 2, 1969, pp.269-277.
14 Martens, *Pierre Mulele, ou, La seconde vie de Lumumba*, p.47.
15 "Lumumba-Mulele-Kabila", *Révolution Congolaise*, No.1, 3 October 2003, p.4, available at www.deboutcongolais.info, accessed 5 June 2019.
16 Founded by Senegalese Alioune Diop in Paris in 1947.
17 Mathew Stanard, "Bilan du monde pour un monde plus déshumanisé": The 1958 Brussels World Fair and Belgian Perceptions of the Congo", *European History Quarterly*, 1 April 2005, Vol.35, Issue 2, pp.267-298.
18 Daniel Boffey, "Belgium comes to terms with 'human zoos' of its colonial past", *The Guardian*, 16 April 2018.
19 Joseph Stalin, *The Foundations of Leninism*, first published in Russian in 1924.
20 Martens, *Pierre Mulele, ou, La seconde vie de Lumumba*, p.52.
21 "Lumumba-Mulele-Kabila", p.4.
22 "Lumumba-Mulele-Kabila", p.4.
23 Herbert F. Weiss, *Political Protest in the Congo: the Parti Solidaire Africain during the Independence Struggle* (Princeton NJ: Princeton University Press, 1967), p.79.
24 The MNC's programme called for immediate independence, and the sudden transition from colony to independent nation is seen as one of the reasons for the subsequent disorder in the Congo.
25 Stephen L. Weigert, *Traditional Religion and Guerilla Warfare in Modern Africa* (New York: St. Martin's Press, 1996), p.51.
26 For the composition of the provincial committee, see Weiss, *Political Protest in the Congo: the Parti Solidaire Africain during the Independence Struggle* (New Jersey: Princeton University Press, 1967), p.92.
27 *Political Protest in the Congo: the Parti Solidaire Africain during the Independence Struggle*, p.95.
28 Verhaegen, *Mulele et la révolution populaire au Kwilu* (Paris: L'Harmattan, 2006), p.38.
29 Fox et al., "The Second Independence": A Case Study of the Kwilu Rebellion in the Congo", p.91.
30 Crawford Young, "Rebellion and the Congo", in Robert I. Rotberg (ed.) *Rebellion in Black Africa* (London: OUP, 1971), p.162.
31 J.S. La Fontaine, *City Politics: A Study of Léopoldville* (Cambridge: At the University Press, 1970), pp.50-51.
32 "Report on the Congo: The diamond smugglers' trail crosses the country and nearly everybody is in the racket", *The Atlantic*, September 1963.
33 Jaques Lavry and Paul Raymaekers, "Conjonctures socio-économiques à Léopoldville", 5e Bulletin, Situation au 15 Décembre 1961, *Notes et Documents*, Vol. II, n° 2/SE-2, (Léopoldville: Université Lovanium, Institut de Recherches Economiques et Sociales), décembre 1961.
34 La Fontaine, *City Politics: A Study of Léopoldville*, p.64.
35 Claude Emerson Welch, *Anatomy of Rebellion* (SUNY Press, 1980), p.197.
36 Claude Emerson Welch, *Anatomy of Rebellion*, p.197.
37 "Congo Police Mutiny Crushed", *The Canberra Times*, 4 May 1963.
38 The Binza Group derives its name from a residential area in Kinshasa. Though the Congolese were forbidden from living in this area during the period of colonisation, on independence rich and influential Congolese soon made it their home and set up a political base. The CIA recognised that the Binza Group could be used as a gateway for American influence in Congolese affairs and actively supported the group's members. Politically opposed to Lumumba, the Binza Group was composed of high-ranking Congolese officials including Mobutu, Foreign Minister Justin Bomboko, Lumumba's Chef de Cabinet, Damien Kandolo, Albert Ndele, the vice-chairman of the College of Commissioners, and Victor Nendaka, the Director of the Sûreté Nationale.
39 Verhaegen, *Mulele et la révolution populaire au Kwilu*, pp.43-44.
40 Verhaegen, *Mulele et la révolution populaire au Kwilu*, p.43.
41 Verhaegen, *Mulele et la révolution populaire au Kwilu*, p.45.
42 *Jeune Afrique*, numéro 172, 24 février, 1964.
43 *Jeune Afrique*, p.46.
44 Martens, *Pierre Mulele, ou, La seconde vie de Lumumba*, pp.134-136.
45 Martens, *Pierre Mulele, ou, La seconde vie de Lumumba*, pp.134-136.
46 "Mao Tse Tung in an interview with a Hsinhua News Agency correspondent, 29 September 1959", and "Mao Tse Tung: Quotations from Mao Tse Tung", Chapter 8. People's War", https://www.marxists.org/reference/archive/mao/works/red-book/ch08.htm, accessed 20 May, 2019.
47 "Mao Tse Tung, *On Protracted War*, Selected Works of Mao Tse Tung, May 1938", https://www.marxists.org/reference/archive/mao/selected-works/volume-2/mswv2_09.htm, accessed 20 May 2019.
48 Bula-Bula, *Pierre Mulele et le maquis du Kwilu en R.D. Congo*, p.32.
49 Verhaegen, *Mulele et la révolution populaire au Kwilu*, p.58.
50 "Lumumba-Mulele-Kabila", p.8.
51 "Lumumba-Mulele-Kabila", p.8.
52 By the 3 September, rumours that Mulele had returned and had set up camps stared to draw the attention of the Kwilu's authorities who promptly put a ransom of 5 million francs on Mulele's head. Government troops were sent to the area to track down Mulele, and if it was suspected that that a village had harboured him, or that villagers had joined the *maquis*, the troops would torture and maim the village's inhabitants. Arms and legs were broken, breasts and ears were cut off, and any clothes, money, or cattle was either stolen, destroyed or killed. Instead of turning the rural population against Mulele and making them divulge his whereabouts, the resolve of villagers hardened, made them hate the ANC even more, and provided them with more reasons to become *maquisards*. Bula-Bula, *Pierre Mulele et le maquis du Kwilu en R.D. Congo*, p.34.

53 Fox et al., "The Second Independence": A Case Study of the Kwilu Rebellion in the Congo", p.101.
54 Fox et al., "The Second Independence": A Case Study of the Kwilu Rebellion in the Congo", p.101.
55 "Lumumba-Mulele-Kabila", p.8.
56 "Lumumba-Mulele-Kabila", p.12.
57 Fox et al., "The Second Independence": A Case Study of the Kwilu Rebellion in the Congo", p.103.
58 Bula-Bula, *Pierre Mulele et le maquis du Kwilu en R.D. Congo*, pp.47-48.
59 Fox et al, "The Second Independence": A Case Study of the Kwilu Rebellion in the Congo", p.96.
60 Fox et al., "The Second Independence": A Case Study of the Kwilu Rebellion in the Congo", p.96.
61 See Michael Massie, "An Analysis of Mao Tse-Tung's Three Main Rules of Discipline and Eight Points for Attention", *American Historical Association Faculty Development Program*, Stony Brook University, 1977, pp.4-5.
62 Fox et al., "The Second Independence": A Case Study of the Kwilu Rebellion in the Congo", p.104.
63 Fox et al., "The Second Independence": A Case Study of the Kwilu Rebellion in the Congo", p.104.
64 "Lumumba-Mulele-Kabila", p.12.
65 "Lumumba-Mulele-Kabila", p.12.
66 Bula-Bula, *Pierre Mulele et le maquis du Kwilu en R.D. Congo*, p.44.
67 "Lumumba-Mulele-Kabila", p.12.
68 Fox et al., "The Second Independence": A Case Study of the Kwilu Rebellion in the Congo", p.104.
69 "Lumumba-Mulele-Kabila", p.12.
70 "Lumumba-Mulele-Kabila", p.12.
71 "Lumumba-Mulele-Kabila", p.12.
72 Verhaegen, *Rebellions au Congo*, pp.126-127, as cited in Weigert, *Traditional Religion and Guerilla Warfare in Modern Africa*, p.58.
73 Weigert, *Traditional Religion and Guerilla Warfare*, p.58.
74 Verhaegen, *Rebellions au Congo*, p.35.
75 Fox et al., "The Second Independence": A Case Study of the Kwilu Rebellion in the Congo", p.100.
76 Weigert, *Traditional Religion and Guerilla Warfare in Modern Africa*, p.58.
77 Weigert, *Traditional Religion and Guerilla Warfare in Modern Africa*, p.58.
78 Weigert, *Traditional Religion and Guerilla Warfare in Modern Africa*, p.58.
79 Weigert, *Traditional Religion and Guerilla Warfare in Modern Africa*, p.59.
80 Weigert, *Traditional Religion and Guerilla Warfare in Modern Africa*, p.59-60.
81 Centre de Recherche et d'Information Socio-Politiques, *Congo 1965* (Brussels: CRISP, 1966) 117 as quoted in Welch, *Anatomy of Rebellion*, p.305.
82 Verhaegen, *Rebellions au Congo*, pp.80-81.
83 Verhaegen, *Rebellions au Congo*, pp.276-277.
84 Benoit Verhaegen, "La rébellion muleliste au Kwilu : chronologie des événements et essai d'interprétation (janvier 1962-juillet 1964)" in C. Coquery-Vidrovitch, A. Forest, and Herbert Weiss (dir.) *Rébellions-Révolution au Zaïre 1963-1965*, (Paris: L'Harmattan, 1987) Tome 1, p.125.
85 "Lumumba-Mulele-Kabila", p.9.
86 Verhaegen, *Rebellions au Congo*, p.277
87 Weigert, *Traditional Religion and Guerilla Warfare in Modern Africa*, p.61.
88 Jules Gerard-Libois and Benoit Verhaegen, *Congo 1965: Political Documents of a Developing Nation* (New Jersey: Princeton University Press, 2015), p.25.
89 Verhaegen, *Rebellions au Congo*, p.278.
90 Verhaegen, *Rebellions au Congo*, p.332.

Chapter 7

1 Herbert Weiss in the introduction to Gerard-Libois and Verhaegen, *Congo 1965: Political Documents of a Developing Nation*.
2 These three provinces were created after Adoula's government restructured the Congo's administrative landscape in 1963.
3 Verhaegen, *Rebellions au Congo*, p.67.
4 Martens, *La seconde vie de Patrice Lumumba*, p.166.
5 Gerard-Libois and Verhaegen, *Political Documents of a Developing Nation*, p.31.
6 Nzongola-Ntalaja, *The Congo from Leopold to Kabila: A People's History*, p.217.
7 Gérard-Libois and Verhaegen, *Political Documents of a Developing Nation*, p.32.
8 Nzongola-Ntalaja, *The Congo from Leopold to Kabila: A People's History*, p.218.
9 Nzongola-Ntalaja, *The Congo from Leopold to Kabila: A People's History*, p.33.
10 A tribal group found in the Kivu.
11 Koen Vlassenroot, *South Kivu: Identity, territory, and power in the eastern Congo* (London: Rift Valley Institute, 2013), p.23.
12 Vlassenroot, *South Kivu: Identity, territory, and power in the eastern Congo*, p.24.
13 Ernesto 'Che' Guevara, *The African Dream: The Diaries of the Revolutionary War in the Congo*, (London: The Harvill Press, 2000), p.6.
14 C. Kabuya-Lumuna Sando, "Laurent Désiré Kabila", *Review of African Political Economy*, Vol.29, No.93/94, September 2002, p.617.
15 David Reed, *111 Days in Stanleyville* (London: Collins, 1966), p.59.
16 "Troops in Congo Fight Ambushers", *New York Times*, 3 May 1964.
17 Gérard-Libois and Verhaegen, *Congo 1965: Political Documents of a Developing Nation*, p.58.
18 Nzongola-Ntalaja, *The Congo from Leopold to Kabila: A People's History*, p.219.
19 "Rebels Hold in Katanga", *The Times*, 26 June, 1964 / "Rebels Seize Congo Town on Border with Burundi", *New York Times*, 18 May 1964 /"Kivu Rebels Rout Troops of Congo", *New York Times*, 1 June, 1964.
20 Reed, *111 Days in Stanleyville*, p.4.
21 Reed, *111 Days in Stanleyville*, p.8.
22 "Fall of Stanleyville to Rebels Reported", *New York Times*, 6 August 1964.
23 "Fall of Stanleyville to Rebels Reported".
24 Reed, *111 Days in Stanleyville*, p.12.
25 Reed, *111 Days in Stanleyville*, p.29.
26 Reed, *111 Days in Stanleyville*, p.31.
27 "Telegram from the Department of State to the Embassy in Belgium", Washington, 28 October 1964, FRUS, Vol. XXIII, Congo, D304.
28 "Telegram from the Department of State to the Embassy in the Congo", Washington, 26 May 1964, FRUS, Vol. XXIII, Congo, D172.
29 "Memorandum for President Johnson", Washington, 15 June 1964, FRUS, Vol. XXIII, Congo, D177.
30 "Memorandum from the Director of the United States Information Agency (Rowan) to President Johnson, Washington, 19 June 1964, FRUS, Vol. XXIII, Congo, D20.
31 "Telegram from the Department of State to the Embassy in Spain", Washington, 22 June 1964, FRUS, Vol. XXIII, Congo, D181.

32 "Memorandum from the Joint Strategic Survey Council to the Joint Chiefs of Staff", Washington, 25 June 1964, FRUS, Vol. XXIII, Congo, D182.

33 "Memorandum From the Under Secretary of State for Political Affairs (Harriman) to the President's Special Assistant for National Security Affairs (Bundy)", Washington, 11 July 1964, FRUS, Vol. XXIII, Congo, D189.

Chapter 8

1 "Telegram From the Department of State to the Embassy in Belgium", Washington, 6 August 1964, FRUS, Vol. XXIII, Congo, D197.

2 "Telegram From the Department of State to the Embassy in Belgium".

3 Verhaegen, *Rebellions au Congo* (Brussels: CRISP, 1966) Vol.1, p.441.

4 Mike Hoare, *Congo Mercenary* (Boulder, CO: Paladin, 2008), p.29.

5 "The Congo: Help Wanted", *Time*, 4 September 1964.

6 Clarke, "The Congo Mercenary: A History and Analysis", p.42.

7 "Men from Many Countries", *The Times*, 23 August 1964.

8 "South Africans Recruited by Congo as Mercenaries", *New York Times*, 24 August 1964.

9 "Rhodesians Signing Up", *New York Times*, 24 August 1964. The identity of the recruiter in Southern Rhodesia is given by Hoare as one 'Patrick O'Malley'. See Hoare, *Congo Mercenary*, p.33.

10 ""Mercenaries" Arrive in Congo", *The Times*, 24 August 1964.

11 Mockler, *Mercenaries*, p.175, and Hoare, *Congo Mercenary*, p.66.

12 Sean Kelly, *America's Tyrant: the CIA and Mobutu of Zaire* (Washington DC: American University Press, 1993), p.142.

13 "Telegram from the Department of State to the Embassy in Kenya", Washington 22 September 1964, FRUS, Vol. XXIII, Congo, D261.

14 "Memorandum from the Deputy Director of the Office of Central African Affairs (Looram) to the Assistant Secretary of State for African Affairs (Williams)", Washington, 19 September 1964, FRUS, Vol. XXIII, Congo, D260.

15 Major Thomas P. Odom, "Dragon Operations: Hostage Rescues in the Congo, 1964-1965", Leavenworth Papers, Number 14, *Combat Studies Institute*, Fort Leavenworth, Kansas, 1986.

16 Vandewalle, *L'Ommegang: Odyssée & Reconquête de Stanleyville, 1964*, pp.148-149.

17 Vandewalle, *L'Ommegang: Odyssée & Reconquête de Stanleyville, 1964*, pp.148-149.

18 Vandewalle, *L'Ommegang: Odyssée & Reconquête de Stanleyville, 1964*, p.172.

19 Vandewalle, *L'Ommegang: Odyssée & Reconquête de Stanleyville, 1964*, p.172.

20 Vandewalle, *L'Ommegang: Odyssée & Reconquête de Stanleyville, 1964*, pp.218-219.

21 According to *Time Magazine*, 27 August 1964, United States aid to the Congo in August 1964 was four C-130 transport planes; three B-26 bombers; ten C-47s; seven F-28s (Fokker short-range airliner); ten helicopters; 70 jeeps; and 250 trucks. According to Fred E. Wagoner, *Dragon Rouge: The Rescue of the Hostages* (University Press of the Pacific, 2003), p.76, seven more B-26s arrived in the Congo in early September 1964.

22 Clarke, "The Congo Mercenary: A History and Analysis", p.47.

23 The collective name given to the forces.

24 Mueller was relieved of his command at Bikili on 12 October 1964. Hoare appointed Rhodesian Ben Louw to replace him. See, Hoare, *Congo Mercenary*, p.81.

25 Hoare, *Congo Mercenary*, p.82-83.

26 Clarke, "The Congo Mercenary: A History and Analysis", pp.45-48, and Frank Villafaña, *Cold War in the Congo: The Confrontation of Cuban Military Forces, 1960-1967* (New Brunswick: Transaction Publishers, 2009), pp.85-86.

27 Villafaña, *Cold War in the Congo: The Confrontation of Cuban Military Forces, 1960-1967*, pp.85-86.

28 Hoare, *Congo Mercenary*, p.76.

29 Lloyd Garrison, "White Mercenaries on a 'Rabbit Hunt'", *New York Times Magazine*, 15 November 1964.

30 Lloyd Garrison, "Tshombe Gains in Battle Against rebels", *New York Times*, 25 October 1964.

31 Hoare, *Congo Mercenary*, pp.76-77.

32 Lloyd Garrison, "Mercenary Group Mutinies in Congo", *New York Times*, 13 October 1964.

33 Villafaña, *Cold War in the Congo: The Confrontation of Cuban Military Forces, 1960-1967*, p.88.

34 Lloyd Garrison, "White Mercenaries Help Retake Key Port in Congo from Rebels", *New York Times*, 8 October 1964.

35 Hoare, *Congo Mercenary*, pp.82-83.

36 "Congo Rebels May Kill Hostages", *New York Times*, 15 October 1964.

37 Footnotes to "Memorandum from the Department of State Executive Secretary (Reed) to the President's Special Assistant for Security Affairs (Bundy)", D285.

38 "Memorandum from the Deputy Director for Plans, Central Intelligence Agency (Helms) to the Under Secretary of State for Political Affairs (Harriman)", 14 October 1964, FRUS, Vol. XXIII, Congo, D284.

39 DEFCON 4, or dense readiness condition 4, refers to the levels of readiness of different strike forces and depends on the severity of a military situation. See, Department of Defense Dictionary of Military and Associated Terms, 12 April 2001, https://web.archive.org/web/20091108082044/http://www.dtic.mil/doctrine/jel/new_pubs/jp1_02.pdf, accessed 4 August 2017.

40 Memorandum from Arthur McCafferty of the National Security Council Staff to the President's Special Assistant for National Security Affairs (Bundy)", *Planning for evacuation of US personnel from Stanleyville*, 15 October 1964, FRUS, Vol. XXIII, Congo, D285.

41 "Memorandum from Arthur McCafferty of the National Security Council Staff to the President's Special Assistant for National Security Affairs (Bundy)".

42 "Memorandum from Arthur McCafferty of the National Security Council Staff to the President's Special Assistant for National Security Affairs (Bundy)".

43 Vandewalle, *L'Ommegang : Odyssée & Reconquête de Stanleyville,1964*, pp.255-256.

44 Vandewalle, *L'Ommegang : Odyssée & Reconquête de Stanleyville,1964*, pp.255-256.

45 Jean-Pierre Sonck, "Opération Dragon Rouge", available at http://www.congo1960.be/Operation_Dragon_Rouge.htm, accessed 22 May 2019.

46 Jean-Pierre Sonck, "Opération Dragon Rouge".

47 The name of the operation was chosen by Colonel Laurent.

48 Sam McGowan, *Anything, Anywhere, Anytime* (Bloomington: AuthorHouse, 2011), p.293.

49 McGowan, *Anything, Anywhere, Anytime*, pp.293-294, and Lowell Hamilton, *Men, Wars and Sex of the 60's*, (Bloomington: Author House, 2017), pp.386-387.

50 "Telegram from the Department of State to the Embassy in Belgium", 16 November 1964, FRUS, Vol. XXIII, Congo, D325.

51 Wagoner, *Dragon Rouge: The Rescue of the Hostages*, p.134.

52 Lloyd Garrison, "Congolese Find Chinese Ammunition Left by Rebels", *New York Times*, 18 November 1964.

53 "Rebel Resistance Light", *New York Times*, 21 November 1964.

54 "Rebels in Congo, Near Showdown, Shift Prisoners", *United Press International*, 22 November 1964.

55 Reed, *111 Days in Stanleyville*, p.160.

56 "Telegram from the Embassy in Kenya to the Department of State", 23 November 1964, FRUS, Vol. XXIII, Congo, D350.
57 "Telegram from the Embassy in the Congo to the Department of State", 21 November 1964, FRUS, Vol. XXIII, Congo, D345.
58 There is some confusion over the exact time of the arrival at Isangi. Although Blanco states that he arrived at 0600, Villafaña states that Blanco was already making strafing passes over Stanleyville airfield at 0545. Some leeway should be accorded when attempting to remember events which took place over 50 years previously. To add further confusion, Belgian historian Jean-Pierre Sonck indicates that the Cubans left Kindu at 04.00, cf. Sonck, "Dragon Rouge".
59 Villafaña, *Cold War in the Congo: The Confrontation of Cuban Military Forces, 1960-1967*, p.98.
60 This is also disputed by McGowan, *Anything, Anywhere, Anytime*, p.294, who gives the take-off time for the C-130's as 0245.
61 Sonck, "Dragon Rouge".
62 Reed, *111 Days in Stanleyville*, p.248.
63 Reed, *111 Days in Stanleyville*, p.249.
64 "Africa: The Congo Massacre", *Time*, 4 December, 1964.
65 Reed, *111 Days in Stanleyville*, p.253.
66 Michèle Timmermans-Zoll, "Mon mari a été abattu sous mes yeux", in "Ce jour-là, 24 novembre 1964: nos paras sautent sur Stanleyville", *Paris Match*, RTBF série, 23 August 2003. Also, personal correspondence with Michèle Timmermans-Zoll.
67 "Africa: The Congo Massacre".
68 Personal correspondence Michèle Timmermans-Zoll, 15 January 2016.
69 Adolf Martin Bormann had become a missionary in the Congo. See, "10 Britons Brought Back to Safety", *The Times*, 25 November, 1964.
70 "Nos Reporteurs au Congo: La Tragedie des Otages", *Paris Match*, No. 817, 5 décembre 1964.

Chapter 9
1 Eliakim Sibanda, *The Zimbabwe African People's Union 1961-1987: A Political History of Insurgency in Southern Rhodesia* (Africa World Press, 2005), p.116.
2 Akyeampong and Gates, *Dictionary of African Biography*, p.466.

Acknowledgements

The completion of this two-volume mini-series would not have been possible without the help of a number of people and organisations in the United Kingdom, France and the United States. In the UK particular thanks go to Chris Kinsey of King's College, London for his advice and, in France my work has been aided not only by individuals such as Robert Houke but also by the library staff of the universities Toulouse 1 Capitol and Toulouse 2 Jean-Jaurès. In the United States, my research has been aided by Carlos Leon Acosta, Manny Pichardo, Roberto Pichardo, Santiago Alvarez, and Felix Rodriguez amongst many other Cuban exiles I have had the pleasure of meeting. Those who I have not met but who have been equally helpful are James Hawes and Frank Villafaña. I am thankful to James Hawes for providing a foreword to the second volume and his patience with my questions. As for Frank Villafaña, his work on Cuban exiles in the Congo is the genesis of much of my own. Thanks go to Helion Publishing and a special mention is given to Tom Cooper. He has provided very useful advice and has guided both projects. My thanks extend to Phil Scoggins for providing valuable information on aircraft design and the same is true of Whirlybirds magazine. Lastly, but not at all least, my thanks go to my wife Deborah for her moral support and patience.

About the Author

Originally from Exeter in Devon, Dr. Stephen Rookes has spent more than half his life living and working in France. He gained his PhD from the University of Toulouse Jean-Jaurès and specialises in the history of the Congo, Cuban exiles and the use of mercenaries in conflict. Rookes is Associate Professor at the Ecole de l'Air (French Air Force Academy) in Salon-de-Provence, and this is his first book for Helion's @War series.